50 WAYS TO PLEASE YOUR LOVER

50 WAYS TO PLEASE YOUR LOVER

WHILE YOU PLEASE YOURSELF

Lonnie Barbach, Ph.D.

A DUTTON BOOK

DUTTON
Published by the Penguin Group
Penguin Books USA Inc., 375 Hudson Street,
New York, New York 10014, U.S.A.
Penguin Books Ltd, 27 Wrights Lane,
London W8 5TZ, England
Penguin Books Australia Ltd, Ringwood,
Victoria, Australia
Penguin Books Canada Ltd, 10 Alcorn Avenue,
Toronto, Ontario, Canada M4V 3B2
Penguin Books (N.Z.) Ltd, 182–190 Wairau Road,
Auckland 10, New Zealand

Penguin Books Ltd, Registered Offices:
Harmondsworth, Middlesex, England

First published by Dutton, an imprint of Dutton Signet,
a division of Penguin Books USA Inc.
Distributed in Canada by McClelland & Stewart Inc.

ISBN 0-525-94271-8 (alk. paper)

Printed in the United States of America
Designed by Michaelis/Carpelis Design Assoc.

Special Thanks

To Udana Power, who contributed the erotic vignettes. Apparent from the stories are Udana's limitless erotic imagination and delightful sense of humor. What may not be apparent, however, are her generosity and lightness of spirit, which have made working with her pure pleasure.

Contents

Introduction xiii

Expanding the Pleasure Realm:
Awakening the Senses 1

   1. Fragrances 3

   2. Aural Sex 6

   3. Oral Sex 9

   4. Topographical "Touch" Map 14

   5. Pubic Art 16

Love Expressed:
Increasing the Love in the Lovemaking . 21

   6. Caring Days 23

   7. Recognition 28

   8. Massage 30

   9. The State of your Union 36

At-Home Specials:
Bringing Passion into the Mundane . . 41

10. Make a Date for Sex 43
11. Take-Out Sex 46
12. The Art of Flirting 48

Truth or Consequences:
Learn Something New About
Your Partner 51

13. Ingredients for Great Sex 53
14. Afterplay 57
15. Upside/Downside 60
16. Erotic Styles 62

Sex Without Intercourse:
Appetizers as the Main Course 65

17. Necking 67
18. His and Her Night 71
19. Foreplay 75
20. The Last Taboo 77

SAFE RISKS:
STEP OUT AND TRY SOMETHING NEW 81

21. SEXUAL INNOVATION 83

22. SEXUAL BREAKOUTS 88

23. RUTLESS RUTTING 90

DRESSING UP OR DRESSING DOWN:
VEILING AND UNVEILING THE BODY
FOR LOVEMAKING 93

24. SEXY UNDERGARMENTS 95

25. THE ART OF UNDRESSING 99

26. THE STRIPTEASE 100

SEX ELSEWHERE:
BROADENING THE SEXUAL BOUNDARIES . . . 107

27. SEX AL FRESCO 109

28. HOT, WET SEX 112

29. TREASURE HUNT 114

SPIRITUAL SEX:

USING SEX TO TOUCH SOULS

USING SEX TO TOUCH SOULS 119

30. Making Love 121

31. Staying on the Edge 126

32. Soul Gazing 130

33. The Blending of Sex and Soul 132

SEX AT A DISTANCE:

WHO SAYS YOU HAVE TO BE IN THE SAME PLACE TO ENJOY SEX?

PLACE TO ENJOY SEX? 135

34. Departures 137

35. Phone Sex 140

THE SEXUAL EDGE:

PUSHING BEYOND SAFE BOUNDARIES

PUSHING BEYOND SAFE BOUNDARIES . . . 145

36. Obstacles as Catalysts 147

37. Transforming Jealousy 151

38. The Hidden Forbidden 153

EROTICA:
ENHANCE YOUR LOVEMAKING WITH WORDS AND IMAGES 157

39. EROTIC VIDEOS 159

40. EROTIC LITERATURE 166

41. HOME VIDEOS 168

FANTASY:
TAKE A BREAK FROM REALITY AND HAVE SOME FUN 171

42. ACT OUT A FANTASY 173

43. SEXUAL REVERIE 177

44. SHARE A FANTASY 178

TOYS:
WHY SHOULD CHILDREN HAVE ALL THE FUN? 187

45. BODY PAINTING 189

46. MÉNAGE À TROIS 192

47. TIE AND TEASE 194

WHEN CONFLICT REARS ITS HEAD:

EVEN GREAT RELATIONSHIPS HAVE
BAD DAYS 201

48. Talking 203

49. Listening 205

50. Conflict Resolution 210

Epilogue 215

Acknowledgments 217

INTRODUCTION

GREAT sex satisfies the body and the soul. It unites a couple in the depths of their beings as they open up fully to the pleasures of their bodies without restraint, embarrassment, or inhibition. Great sex can also nourish intimacy in other aspects of the relationship.

50 Ways to Please Your Lover: While You Please Yourself is designed to "stimulate" your sexual relationship in the best sense of the word. Whether you have been lovers for 50 days or 50 years, this book will add spice, range, and play to your lovemaking.

There are many ways to use this book: If you are methodical and don't like to miss anything, you might start with the first activity and end with the last one—making certain to enjoy each and every suggestion along the way. Or, on the spur of the moment, you could open the book to a page at random and see where the activity leads you, or pick a category that turns you on and "play" within that area. You might want to read the vignettes aloud to your partner as a part of your lovemaking or, instead, you could choose to read the book alone, both to keep your sexual energy simmering and as a way to store up ideas to try out at some future date. You could agree with your partner to carry out one new activity each week to add novelty to your sex life. You could also take the volume with you on a weekend away or give it as an anniversary, birthday, or Valentine's gift as a way to initiate some innovative sexual fun.

The most important thing is to see the adventure in your sexual relationship and to have fun with it. Feel free to change and adapt the suggestions in this book to your own special needs and interests. View it as a jumping off place for your own sexual creativity. And if you develop some great new sexual ideas on your own, send them to me to be included in a sequel. The possibilities for a deeper and richer intimate life are nearly infinite.

Meanwhile, enjoy yourself thoroughly.

Lonnie Barbach, Ph.D.
c/o Dutton Books
375 Hudson St.
New York, NY 10014

50 WAYS TO PLEASE YOUR LOVER

50 WAYS TO PLEASE YOUR LOVER

AWAKENING THE SENSES

1. FRAGRANCES

◆ ◆ ◆ ◆ ◆ ◆ ◆ ◆ ◆ ◆ ◆ ◆ ◆ ◆ ◆

JAMES picked up the message from his voice mail; Sarah would meet him in front of the Ivy at four-thirty. As he walked across the patio from the gym after his workout he saw her standing there next to the white picket fence. She was wearing that romantic little loose-fitting dress that was so impossibly sexy. Without saying a word, she reached for his hand and led him down the street. She stopped at a small shop with two names on the door and grinned as she led him inside, then watched his expression as he reacted to his surroundings.

It was the subtlety of the fragrances that he liked most. Nothing obvious but definitely strong . . . the wonderful smells seemed to relax and quiet as well as stimulate him. Beauty was everywhere. The bottles of potions and oils and soaps were packaged with natural twine and dried flowers. The soft lighting in the store was enhanced by the fragrant candles that flickered in their ceramic holders and shed dancing stars and moons on the walls. This place was magical.

James and Sarah spent over an hour and a half in the small shop, smelling, testing, exploring, and tantalizing each other with intimations of the evening ahead. The way Sarah looked at him from across the room, her face so vulnerable yet erotic, made him want to make love to her right there. He wondered if the salesperson could tell what they were up to. He glanced around, but she was busy helping someone else.

When he turned back to Sarah, she was approaching him like a vision. He felt as though he had dropped through a time warp into a world devoted to the senses. She held out the tender inside of her wrist for him to smell. "Which one do you like?" she asked. He took her delicate hand in his and inhaled deeply. The fragrance seemed to go right down to his toes and mingle with his love for her. Just then the world disappeared, leaving only the two of them, their love, and the scent of *China Rain*.

While individual pheromones are the original aphrodisiacs, adding scent to lovemaking can create an additional spark.

- *Spray or dab perfume or cologne on your wrists, neck, and especially your inner thighs.*
- *Light a scented candle or some incense.*
- *Use a fragrant soap to shower or bathe.*
- *Massage your partner's body with a scented body oil.*

Go together to purchase a soap, oil, perfume, or candle with a fragrance you both enjoy and use it to enhance your lovemaking.

◆

To discover the richness of this often overlooked sexual stimulant, focus on your sense of smell the next time you make love.

◆

2. Aural Sex

◆ ◆ ◆ ◆ ◆ ◆ ◆ ◆ ◆ ◆ ◆ ◆ ◆

THEY stood chatting about nothing in a line that started under the old-fashioned marquee, strung itself down the block like a lazy snake of human bodies, and wrapped around the corner. Suddenly something happened to the tone of his voice. It got low and husky and filled with such richness that it warmed her inside and made her tingle.

"I love you, honey." He gazed steadily into her eyes, his lids heavy with sex. "I love you and want to be inside you right now."

She glanced up in surprise. He turned her around and wrapped his arms around her so that her body "spooned" against his, then leaned in close to her ear and whispered, "I want to feel myself inside you. I want to feel you wet and warm around my cock. And then I'm going to move slowly in and out, again and again, for a long, long time so you can come and come and come. I love to watch you come, baby . . ." He groaned with the pleasure of his thoughts.

She felt him grow hard against the small of her back as he gently pressed himself against her. She glanced at the other people standing in line; could anyone tell? No, they were just another couple waiting for the movie. He put his lips close to her ear and continued as though telling a secret. She closed her eyes and smiled as she let her body relax back into his. She reached up for his head and gently brought his ear down next to her lips and whispered, "I love your cock. I love to feel it hard and hot inside me. I love it when you fuck me deep and talk dirty."

Talk down and dirty; recite love poems—aural lovemaking can accentuate your turn-on. For example:

◆ *Whisper "I love you" as you kiss his ear.*

- Tell her "You feel so good to me" as you fondle her breasts.
- Let your partner know how beautiful/handsome she/he is to you when nude.
- Say, "I want you inside me" / "I want to be inside you."
- Say, "Harder!"
- Say, "Don't stop!"

Some people are particularly turned on by the use of four-letter words, the raunchier the better.

◆

Before deciding on the relative benefits or liabilities of aural sex, experiment with a variety of sex talk to discover what works for both of you.

◆

3. ORAL SEX

JOSHUA'S callused hands cupped her small, firm breasts as he kissed down her belly to the patch of fur between her legs. "Oh, my God," she thought. "He's going to do it."

She was nervous and found it hard to relax. His tongue brushed across the tender folds of her vulva. Then it flicked back and forth on the little swollen knob that stood guard at the doorway to the center of her being. She heard a muffled sigh as he pressed his tongue into her, then circled it back to her clit and stroked back and forth again and again.

It felt wonderful, and yet she worried. Did she taste okay? Would his tongue hit the right place? And for long enough?

He continued burrowing between her legs. He seemed to love it. His strong hands stroked her thighs and then pressed her legs apart so that he could push his lips and tongue even deeper. His tongue flicked back and forth across the little bud that kept swelling with desire. He didn't stop. He kept pressing his tongue in a gentle rhythm that she began to trust and surrender to. And the more she released and relaxed into his steady stimulation, the closer she came to the edge of orgasm.

She felt his fingers move up inside her vagina. They slipped in and out as his tongue continued to pulse back and forth. He didn't stop. He didn't change. He just continued on and on, allowing her to relax deeper and deeper into her feelings until suddenly she felt herself spill over the edge. She was falling and blooming at the same time. The energy burst up from that little bud nestled against his tongue; the muscles pressed and pulsed around his fingers, contracting again and again. Excitement poured out onto his face; he groaned and continued sucking and licking with even more intensity. She cried out; her body arched. He moaned as he rode the wave of her orgasm with her. His lips and mouth stayed on her until the wave subsided and she came to rest. She held his head still ... her clit was so sensitive she didn't want him to move, just to lie there with her until she could come back to this planet.

Take a bath or shower together. Relax and enjoy the sensations of soaping your partner's body.

Experiment. Spread a towel over your bedsheet or a chair seat and apply one of these to your partner's genitals:

- *whipped cream*
- *chocolate sauce*
- *flavored syrups*
- *flavored edible massage oils*

Assume a comfortable position and then lick the substance off. Even when the sauce, syrup, or cream is gone, continue to suck, tongue, and nibble your partner's genitals.

FELLATIO

♦ If you do not want your partner to ejaculate in your mouth, ask him to signal you verbally or by touching your head or shoulder just before he is ready to ejaculate so you can remove his penis from your mouth.

♦ To prevent your partner's penis from going too far into your mouth, encircle the base of his penis with your hand. This will act as a buffer. To intensify his pleasure, firmly stroke his penis with your hand as you suck on him.

CUNNILINGUS

- If you are concerned about odor, dab some of your favorite perfume on your partner's pubic hair or inner thigh—but not inside the outer lips (alcohol can burn mucosal tissue).

- Maintaining a firm and steady rhythm, through to the end of the orgasm, is critical for most women.

---◆---

Next to the hand, the mouth-lips-tongue area is the most manipulable part of the human body, making oral sex particularly pleasurable. Saliva is an excellent natural sexual lubricant.

---◆---

4. TOPOGRAPHICAL "TOUCH" MAP

◆ ◆ ◆ ◆ ◆ ◆ ◆ ◆ ◆ ◆ ◆ ◆ ◆ ◆ ◆

WARM up the room. Get out paper and your favorite pencils, paints, or markers and study your partner's genitals. Then draw your vision of them. Don't worry about your artistic ability.

After you finish the drawing, touch the different areas of your partner's genitals and elicit a response from 1 to 5 in terms of sensitivity. A 1 would mean that the area is quite insensitive to touch; a 5 would mean it is extremely sensitive.

Choose a different color for each of the five numbers on the scale. Then color each area of your drawing with the color that corresponds to the appropriate sensitivity level. When you are finished, you will have created a unique sensitivity topographical map of your partner's genitals—and you may also have learned something new about this special area of your partner's body.

Switch roles so that each of you have the opportunity to be both artist and model.

———————◆———————

Creating a good likeness is less important than allowing your creative expression and other energies to flow forth freely.

———————◆———————

5. PUBIC ART

❖ ❖ ❖ ❖ ❖ ❖ ❖ ❖ ❖ ❖ ❖ ❖ ❖

HE had always loved Georgia O'Keeffe's paintings. Her images were organic. Natural. And totally erotic. These were his thoughts as he sat in front of Samantha's cunt and stroked the unruly hair.

Samantha sat on the kitchen counter, leaning back against the cupboard. Her feet rested against the tiles and her legs were spread open before him. *"A masterpiece,"* he thought to himself as he pulled out a small comb and gently ran it through the thatch of deep brown hair.

"Do you mind if I trim it?" he asked politely.

She smiled as she looked down at him. "Of course not. You can do what you like." Her eyelids fell to half-mast as she gazed at him. "You do make me feel like a work of art."

"That's because you are one," he responded as he produced a small pair of scissors and began to trim the wispy edges.

Soon the thick mass of hair was transformed into a small circular tuft and he saw those vulnerable lips up close. He had never seen a woman's vulva so clearly. The love place. The cunt. The doorway to paradise. The come-to-me-and-lose-your-heart-and-soul place.

He spread the lips gently to see the deep pink passionflower that he had made love to so many times. Funny, he had never carefully looked at it before. He spread the lips and gazed at the pleasure spot. Yes, it really did look like a Georgia O'Keeffe painting. He wanted to lick it, to stick his tongue in between those pink petals, but he restrained himself. He just stared at the delicacy of that incredibly private place and marveled at its power and perfection.

Then he reached over Samantha's leg to the pots of

finger paints sitting next to her on the counter. He dipped two fingers into the turquoise and carefully stroked down her inner thigh from the dark tufted center, as though he were creating a stem for her perfect passionflower. Then he realized that he needed yellow and pink and red and violet . . . for the energy emanating from this secret doorway was vibrant, electric, and filled with power. He put his fingers into the other jars of thick paint and spread colorful petals on her abdomen. Then he traced rays of bright sunshine out from their source of life between her legs up to her belly and down over her hips.

Samantha dropped her head back and sighed with pleasure. Feeling his hands tenderly stroke thick finger paints all over her most vulnerable parts was unexpectedly arousing.

His finger painting was deliciously childlike and free. Vibrant primary colors coursed down her inner thighs like tendrils of electric energy. The still life wasn't professional. It wasn't even particularly good. But it was wonderful. Long before he could capture what he was trying to capture, he put his arms around her legs and moved his face in close so that his tongue could explore those beautiful folds. Now his tongue knew where it was going—the inner lips, the little bud tucked in its secret place, and the rose-colored opening muscle that was his gate to heaven.

A pubic coiffure mixes creativity, intimacy, and fun.
  Gather together:

- *a pair of scissors*
- *a safety razor*
- *a small comb*
- *watercolors, finger paints, or colored water-based, nontoxic markers*

Then take turns designing and cutting your partner's pubic area until it assumes the image you have in mind.

- Add color with markers or paints and create a tattoo-like work of art.
- Some people like to shave their partner's pubic hair off completely.

After executing your design, have fun making love to the image you have created.

◆

Newly cut or shaved hair can feel scratchy while growing in, but discomfort generally disappears after a few days. Applying soothing lotion can reduce irritation.

◆

INCREASING THE LOVE IN THE LOVEMAKING

6. CARING DAYS

◆ ◆ ◆ ◆ ◆ ◆ ◆ ◆ ◆ ◆ ◆ ◆ ◆ ◆

IT was the most expensive suit Ben had ever bought. Ginger helped him pick it out. She was right; he felt like a million dollars, and it made an impact on the board. They listened to him differently.

As he left the meeting, his hand reached unconsciously into his jacket pocket. Something was in it. He pulled it out. A black nylon with a seam down the back. "My baby knows how to stoke the fire," he said to himself with a grin.

When he got to his office he went directly to the top drawer of his desk and pulled out a neatly typed list. He caressed his face with the black silk nylon as he read:

Things I Adore:

◆ Call me just to tell me you love me.

- Reach for my hand in a crowd.
- Daisies.
- Let me know you're thinking about me.
- A small gift now and then.
- Cunnilingus.
- Kissing me on the back of the neck.
- Massaging my feet.
- Noticing what I wear.
- Holding me in your arms.
- Surprising me with a video.
- Sexy E-mail.

And the list went on. It had been added to in pencil and in pen. He chose "Daisies" for openers. He speed-dialed the nursery and had them deliver two large red pots with white and yellow daisies blooming their heads off. Great for the deck. Then he sat at his computer and pulled up E-mail. He took a moment to think of her, then wrote: "I have a nylon here that longs to be on your gorgeous leg and stroked by me. I'm feeling very sexy thinking of you. When I get home I plan to make love to you outside on the chaise near the flowers and under the stars. Love, Ben."

Feeling truly cared for by your partner can make you more loving and turned on. Often, we try to show our caring by doing for our partner those things we'd like our partner to do for us—like cooking a great meal or bringing home flowers—and hope our lover will thereby get the hint. However, hinting may not always be effective.

Instead, be direct. Think about some simple things that your partner does or could do—both in and out of the bedroom—that make you feel cared for. Then write them down in a list.

For example:

♦ *Calling me during the day.*
♦ *Kissing me good-bye.*
♦ *Planning a night on the town.*
♦ *Complimenting me on how I look.*
♦ *Calling me "Darling" [or some other specific term of endearment].*
♦ *Hugging me often.*

All the items on the list should be positive—things you would like your partner to start to do or continue to do. Chores like cleaning the cat box are off-limits. Also off-limits are things you want your partner to stop doing like "Stop calling me from the top of the stairs" or "Stop taking phone calls at mealtime."

Then discuss each of your Caring Days lists in detail. Talk about what each item means and why it makes you feel cared for.

As a gentle reminder, post both of your lists on the medicine cabinet, the bathroom mirror, or some other visible place.

To keep your relationship thriving, carrying out two items on your partner's list every day.

———————◆———————

Make the lists as long as possible. Keep adding items as the days and weeks go by. A longer list means greater variety and more options from which to choose.

———————◆———————

7. RECOGNITION

♦ ♦ ♦ ♦ ♦ ♦ ♦ ♦ ♦ ♦ ♦ ♦ ♦ ♦ ♦ ♦

We all want to feel appreciated by our mate and recognized for what we contribute. When we feel appreciated, we feel more loving and more generous. It is uniquely human to delight in praise and attention.

Take time to think of one or two things your partner did over the previous twenty-four hours that you appreciated, such as:

♦ taking out the garbage
♦ cooking a great dinner
♦ cleaning the cat box
♦ phoning just to say "Hello"
♦ rubbing your head before you went to sleep
♦ noticing that you cleaned the garage

Pick a specific time each day to share your appreciations of each other. At breakfast, when you return home from work, at dinner, or when you get into bed in the evening are all good potential times.

———◆———

Continue to appreciate your partner daily for the rest of your lives. Love not expressed is love not conveyed—the thought alone is not sufficient.

———◆———

8. MASSAGE

◆ ◆ ◆ ◆ ◆ ◆ ◆ ◆ ◆ ◆ ◆ ◆ ◆

THE silk robe felt cool and delicious against her skin. She tied it loosely and thought of geishas, women of centuries past whose primary purpose in life was to pleasure men. For some reason the thought turned her on.

When he walked in the front door he looked tired. Spent. He appeared wary of anyone who might make demands. Even her. Especially for sex.

She smiled and said, "I have a surprise for you."

She led him into the bedroom. It was warm, the light from scented candles flickered on the walls and Chopin's Nocturnes played softly in the background. He stopped, unsure of what would be required of him. She took his jacket and soothed, "You don't have to do anything but relax, darling. I'm going to thoroughly enjoy you."

He looked down at her, surprised and intrigued.

She added, "All you have to do is lie there. I have the magic balm." She held up the massage oil. "You just relax, fall asleep, zone out, bliss away . . . and let me have my way with your body. It's better than a martini."

He finally heaved a sigh and slumped down on the edge of the bed. As she took off his shoes, he fell backward and stretched his arms out. It felt so good to be touched. Just to be touched.

She helped him remove every last stitch of clothing, then turned him over onto his stomach. He quietly groaned with appreciation as her bare legs straddled his butt; the softness of her thighs felt good against his skin. She spurted a small amount of warm oil into her palm and rubbed her hands together before she placed them on his back. He drifted out into euphoria as her hands began to stroke him.

She spent half an hour exploring every nook and cranny of his body with massage oil. She rubbed his neck, his shoulder blades, under his arms, down his back, and the mounds of his muscular butt. She explored the mysterious crack that led to the base of his scrotum, where his legs were joined. She lingered there awhile, then stroked massage oil down his long legs and squished her slippery fingers between each of his toes. Then she turned him over and started on the front. From his forehead to his eyebrows and ears to his lips . . . down his pectoral muscles. She traced the line of hair from his navel to his cock, then let her hands stroke and pleasure his soft penis. She put more oil in her hands and stroked his balls. His penis hardened a little, so she kissed the dome of its bald head, then continued on her adventure down the insides of his thighs to his knees and the front of his shins until she, once again, arrived at his toes. By the time she was done she had slipped her fingers in and out of every possible crevice. He was sound asleep.

She removed her silk robe and stretched out alongside his strong body and wrapped her leg over his. He snuggled his body closer to hers and together they drifted off to sleep.

The object of a caring massage is to soothe, relax, and explore the potential for sensual awakening— not to work out muscle kinks.

Prepare an environment where you won't be disturbed. You should be warm, comfortable, and secure.

◆ *Close the shades.*
◆ *Add some flowers.*
◆ *Light a candle or two.*
◆ *Turn on pleasant music.*
◆ *Lie on the rug or on a firm bed freshly made up with your favorite sheets.*

- *And don't forget talcum powder or a bottle of oil; both can enhance the pleasure of a caring massage. The oil or powder should have a light, pleasant scent that you both enjoy.*

Make sure you have everything you need at hand— once you start you won't want to be interrupted.

As "Giver"

- *Spend thirty minutes experiencing and stroking your partner's body in a loving way that gives you pleasure. Don't overemphasize breasts and genitals, but don't avoid them either.*

As "Receiver"

- *Relax and enjoy the massage. If a certain kind of touching feels unpleasant to you, let your partner know in a positive way how it could be changed. For example, say "A little more firmly, please; that* tickles." If the touch is neutral or pleasurable, simply relax and enjoy it.

After thirty minutes, switch roles and reverse roles on another occasion and spend the additional time extending the massage into something more risqué.

◆

The skin is the largest sense organ. Touch is important to the health and well-being of all mammals. Find occasion to touch your partner lovingly at least a few times every day.

◆

9. THE STATE OF YOUR UNION

LEE poured two glasses of Chablis while Kate dimmed the lights and turned down the phone.

"Don't forget the answering machine. Turn off the voice."

"It's done," said Kate as she settled down next to him on the overstuffed sofa.

He handed her a glass, they clinked and took a sip, then Lee looked at her intently and said, "The State of our Union is now open for discussion."

Kate snuggled close to him so that she could feel the warmth of his strong body. She was unsure how she was going to say what she had been avoiding for days.

He interrupted her thoughts. "Tell me what you don't want to say," he said.

Kate gulped down her panic as she set the wineglass on the table next to her. She avoided his eyes.

"That's the one I want to know." He gently tipped her face toward him.

"Well . . ." she began hesitantly, "I've just been feeling . . . I mean . . . I know you've been busy . . . but . . . It's just that I'd like . . ."

"Just say it, Kate. I'm not going anywhere. I'm a big boy."

"Okay. . . ." Finally she looked him square in the eyes and said what was on her mind. "I miss you. Even when you're here, you're not here. We don't make love enough. Doing it in the dark in the middle of the night when we're both really tired doesn't make me feel loved or cherished. And I want to feel loved and cherished. By you."

There. She had said it. She looked him straight in the eyes. He was a little taken aback. She hoped against hope that this wouldn't start an argument.

He sat thoughtfully perplexed for a moment, then suddenly grinned. "Okay." He caressed her face as he considered a solution. "But right now you know the schedule I'm under. Can I love and cherish you for ten minutes at a time and then go back to concentrating on my work? Until I close this deal."

"Ten minutes is all I need. I just want to know I still matter to you. I know you're busy, but when days go by and I feel ignored, I start to withdraw and get angry."

"That's an easy fix. I got it." He kissed her lightly on the mouth. "The deal closes next week; after that you and I can go away for a weekend. But I have a request."

"Yes?"

"I don't want to go on an exercise weekend. I don't want to hear about being healthy or hiking or counting fat grams. I just want to eat. And lie round. And let you give me great head. And, by the way, I loved the way you woke me up last Thursday. I thought about it all day."

"You did?" Kate grinned as she relaxed into his arms.

Set aside an hour to talk with your partner about the State of your Union. Share your feelings on where you think the relationship is heading and what rough spots need to be ironed out.

End the discussion by letting your partner know three things that he or she did for you during the previous week that you particularly appreciated.

◆

Whether you are married or not, you could use this opportunity to exchange vows or words of intention that are appropriate for your relationship in the present. Periodic conversations about the State of your Union are a good idea for all intimate relationships.

◆

BRINGING PASSION INTO THE MUNDANE

10. MAKE A DATE FOR SEX

◆ ◆ ◆ ◆ ◆ ◆ ◆ ◆ ◆ ◆ ◆ ◆ ◆ ◆

ALAN took a bite of toast and gulped down his coffee as the kids came tearing into the room. Anne herded them toward the breakfast table as she reached for the milk and a large assortment of dry cereals. With two kids under ten, things just never seemed to quiet down.

Alan grabbed his laptop and jacket and hurried for the back door. Anne rushed to intercept him: "Hey, Honey . . . how'd you like a hot date on Sunday morning?"

Alan's face brightened as he turned back to her. Suddenly the noise of the kids and the turmoil of his day ahead faded into the background. Anne moved closer and continued seductively. "You know, Mom said she'd take the kids to soccer on Sunday morning . . ."

Alan smiled at the thought. "That would give us two hours alone . . ." he said.

"Or even four, if I give her money for pizza," she added. "I can massage your feet until you turn into a puddle of bliss . . ." His eyes lit up at the thought. "I can even make us breakfast in bed," she continued.

"I'll have *you* for breakfast in bed," he said, kissing her full on the mouth. "It's a date. Carve it in stone."

Alan looked over her shoulder at the two bundles of wild energy slapping milk and Cheerios all over the table. He looked back at his wife and smiled as he leaned down to kiss her gently.

There was a lightness to his step and a twinkle in his eye as he hurried to the old Volvo station wagon. How could something so simple make him feel so happy? A date with his wife . . . he grinned at the thought. It still got him excited.

For most people, appointments with friends or busi-ness colleagues or family obligations, fill appoint-

ment books, and intimate relationships are relegated to last place.

To rejuvenate your sex life, schedule intimate time first. Together, set a date and time in the next week to spend romantically together and write it on your calendar. Then protect and honor it.

Plan ahead so you can look forward to the time together. Think of something to do to make it special—wear some sexy clothing, open a bottle of champagne—as you would for a weekend away or a birthday celebration. Then enjoy each other to the fullest.

◆

Make dates with your partner more sacred than business meetings—otherwise your business will thrive while your relationship falters.

◆

11. TAKE-OUT SEX

◆ ◆ ◆ ◆ ◆ ◆ ◆ ◆ ◆ ◆ ◆ ◆ ◆ ◆

All too often, we don't make love until late at night, when we're exhausted. After finishing a hard day's work and evening chores there may be little time to connect on an emotional level, and the sex that follows can feel perfunctory or even unpleasant.

To remedy this situation, choose a night when one of you can pick up pizza, hamburgers, Chinese food, sandwiches, or some other take-out dinner.

When you get home from work, jump into bed—with or without clothes on. (If you have young children, get into bed right after putting them to sleep.) Talk while you picnic between the sheets.

◆ *Keep the conversation on a positive note.*
◆ *Steer away from criticism and conflicts.*
◆ *Express your loving feelings toward each other.*

◆ *Share your hopes and long-term goals.*
◆ *Stay connected physically by touching arms, legs, and feet.*

Turn the lights low, and savor your partner for dessert.

———————◆———————

I know a couple who have what they call "chop suey night" every Tuesday.

———————◆———————

12. THE ART OF FLIRTING

◆ ◆ ◆ ◆ ◆ ◆ ◆ ◆ ◆ ◆ ◆ ◆ ◆ ◆

THE pool party was in full swing. Kids ran around squealing with delight. Rob watched Ed man the barbecue while Susan stretched out on the chaise across the patio and sunned herself. Rob had been keeping an eye on Susan even while engrossed in conversation with Ed. He loved the way she watched him out of the corner of her eyes while she smoothed lotion all over her body. A deliberate turn-on. When she leaned back to sunbathe she looked magnificent.

Suddenly she wasn't there. Rob immediately forgot about Ed and looked around; Ed stopped in mid-hamburger flip to follow Rob's gaze.

"Sorry, Ed. I . . ."

Just then Rob felt a hand slip into his back pocket. He turned to see Susan, wearing a straw hat and a gauzy shirt over her bikini.

"Don't let me interrupt. I just came by to check out the meat," she said huskily, looking hypnotically into Rob's eyes. "Continue on with your conversation."

"This I gotta see," said Ed, laughing. "A man who can carry on a conversation standing next to a beautiful, half-naked woman with her hand in his pocket. Sure."

Feeling sexually attractive is essential to exciting sex. Flirting instills this feeling—after all, that's probably how you became increasingly attracted to your mate in the first place. Flirting is a way to say "I feel alive sexually—especially with you."

Some flirting techniques from the subtle to the not-so-subtle:

- *Tell your partner how good he or she looks to you.*
- *Sensuously and surreptitiously stroke your partner's backside.*

- ◆ *Give your partner a good-bye kiss he or she won't forget.*
- ◆ *In a sexy voice, ask your partner if he or she is busy after dinner.*

Find two ways to flirt with your partner today.

———————◆———————

To enliven your relationship, keep flirtation a part of your daily regime.

———————◆———————

LEARN SOMETHING NEW ABOUT YOUR PARTNER

13. Ingredients for Great Sex ◆◆◆◆◆◆◆◆◆◆◆◆◆◆

HE drove. She manned the radio as they sped down the highway. They were both mesmerized by the interview they had just heard. When the host went to commercial break Eliza switched off the radio and asked Nick the same question the psychologist had asked.

"So, Nick . . . remember, no last names . . . can you tell us . . . what is your favorite sexual pleasure?" She held her breath waiting for his answer.

Nick kind of choked and cleared his throat. "You kidding?"

"No, Nick. You're live on 102-point-3 FM. Nobody knows your last name. You can speak freely. Tell us . . . what is it that you prefer to all else?"

Nick seemed to have a hard time deciding. "Well . . . I . . . ah . . ."

She tried to help. "Fellatio? Cunnilingus? Doing it in the elevator? Doggie style in the kitchen?"

Nick chuckled and shook his head, then replied, "Well, I gotta tell ya . . . my favorite is kissing. Just plain kissing." Eliza was shocked. Truly. Could it be as simple as that?

He continued. "Yeah . . . I don't know . . . there's something about it . . . that's really erotic. I mean . . . there's all that tenderness . . . like you're peeking into someone's heart . . . I mean . . . it's really personal . . . you can't make out with someone you don't really care for. It's like you're unwrapping this wonderful present . . . it's . . . I don't know. . . . All that other locker room stuff is just that . . . locker-room stuff. I like kissing."

Well, you could have knocked Eliza over with a feather, but she wasn't one to miss a cue. "So, Nick, I notice that there's a view stop up ahead. Why don't you just pull in and describe to our listening audience all those things you like about kissing. In detail. Give us a little lesson here. You can take as much time as you like; we have all day. . . ."

And Nick pulled the Mustang off the road so that he and Eliza could get in a little practice.

Each and every one of us is unique sexually. To learn more about your partner's distinctive sexual preferences and to enable your partner to learn more about yours, make a list of ten items that heighten a sexual experience for you. Then exchange your lists.

For example:

◆ *Having at least an hour of available time.*
◆ *Feeling rested.*
◆ *Hard stimulation of the penis/gentle clitoral stroking.*
◆ *Having toes sucked.*

- *Firm pulling of hair.*
- *Rock music.*
- *Sex in the living room on the rug in front of the fire.*

The next time you make love, integrate two of the items on your partner's list into the experience.

———◆———

Don't forget to include in your list one or two items you consider a little weird or kinky. These are likely to be among the most important.

———◆———

14. AFTERPLAY

◆ ◆ ◆ ◆ ◆ ◆ ◆ ◆ ◆ ◆ ◆ ◆ ◆ ◆ ◆ ◆

HE was lost in her again and wanted to be even deeper inside. His body took over and continued to pump harder and harder. He wanted to melt into her pores and saturate every cell of her body. She held her clit against his penis so that each thrust would bring her closer to orgasm. He loved it when she did that . . . and he loved when they came together.

He cried out as the force came right up from the base of his balls and took him over. He arched his back and felt the surge of energy pour up through his cock and explode into her body. She gasped and let out a deep moan. A blast of warmth seemed to burst out of her and envelop him. He thrust himself inside her one last time before he fell forward and clung to her as they spun out through space together. Hurtling through eons and galaxies . . . somewhere out on the edge of eternity where time stands still. These were the moments when nothing else mattered. These were the times when it all made sense . . . when he was inside her.

They floated out there for a long time . . . as though they had dropped through a hole in space. When they finally came back, his penis was flaccid, but his heart was vibrating with love for her. He kissed her cheek gently and lifted himself away. Her dark hair swirled on the pillow like a wild woman's. He motioned for her to stay there and went into the bathroom, where he soaked a clean washcloth in warm water. He brought it back with a fluffy hand towel and sat down next to where she lay and gently wiped all his love juice from between her legs. The warm towel caressed the pink folds of her pussy. He loved giving her pleasure. Her body stretched out luxuriously and she sighed. How could it be that touching that love space with his cock could cause such pleasure? It didn't matter how . . .

just that it did. He cupped her with the fluffy towel and gently dried the treasure, then lay down beside her to tell her how much he loved her.

There is no better way to end a sexual experience than to prolong the intimate feelings. Think of ways you can extend those loving moments.

◆ *Give or receive a light back-scratch or gentle massage.*
◆ *Cuddle in spoon position with his hand on her breast or her hand on his cock.*
◆ *Have a verbal instant replay of how great the sex was.*
◆ *Talk about how much you love each other.*

Discuss five afterplay activities you would each enjoy. Try one of them after you make love next time and every time thereafter.

———————◆———————

As love deepens, afterplay becomes foreplay for the next sexual experience.

———————◆———————

15. UPSIDE/DOWNSIDE

◆ ◆ ◆ ◆ ◆ ◆ ◆ ◆ ◆ ◆ ◆ ◆ ◆ ◆ ◆

OFTEN, the behavior we find the hardest to deal with in our mates is really the downside of an aspect that we treasure in them. For example:

◆ *You may love his carefree spirit but be annoyed with his irresponsibility.*

◆ *You may love her warmth and generosity but find she gives so much to others that you don't feel enough is left over for you.*

◆ *You may respect his take-charge attitude but resent his bossiness.*

◆ *You may count on her interest and personal support but become exasperated by all of her questions.*

Tell your partner five aspects of his or her personality that you like the most. Then pick one that you like the least and explain why it bothers you.

Explore together how this attribute might be the downside of one of the personality traits you appreciate. And the next time your partner does something that upsets you, try to keep the upside of that negative trait in mind.

———————◆———————

No positives exist in life without their attendant negatives.

———————◆———————

16. EROTIC STYLES

◆ ◆ ◆ ◆ ◆ ◆ ◆ ◆ ◆ ◆ ◆ ◆ ◆

PERSONALS: *Women Seeking Men*

WANTED: A man who is brilliant, passionate, intense, and loving. Tall, creative, with a tender heart, and who loves to kiss. A man who likes to experiment and explore and make love in new places. A wild man who sets off my fireworks and loves to cherish me. . . . He is the man of my dreams.

As if you were completing an erotic personals ad, write a short description of the most positive aspects of your partner as a sexual being. For example:

◆ *The way she uses her tongue so deftly.*
◆ *His soft yielding kisses.*

◆ *The way she struts.*
◆ *His aroma.*

Now read your descriptions to each other as a kind of love letter. Sometimes sexual attributes are overlooked when appreciations are expressed. Directly discussing them opens another area of intimate communication—and communication is what intimacy is built on.

———————◆———————

Sexual attributes can be as important as intellect or personality.

———————◆———————

APPETIZERS AS THE MAIN COURSE

17. NECKING
◆ ◆ ◆ ◆ ◆ ◆ ◆ ◆ ◆ ◆ ◆ ◆ ◆ ◆ ◆

IT was Lainie's forty-fifth birthday party. She invited all her old high school buddies who still lived close enough to attend, rented a jukebox with all the old songs, pulled out a cashmere sweater set, and actually found a poodle skirt at a thrift shop. Thanks to a low-fat diet, she looked almost teenagey (if she stood far enough away from the mirror and didn't wear her glasses). Peter still had his varsity sweater, minus a few holes the moths had enjoyed.

The sound of Sam Cooke singing "You Send Me" filled the air as Vernette walked in with Roy, both dressed in their old teenage stuff. They squealed with delight and jumped up and down when they saw each other. Soon Muffy and Steve arrived on a double date with Sam and Dodie. Deborah Zalk entered with her new husband; she was still the prettiest woman around.

And Suzie Bonnett no longer had the smallest waist, but who cared? They were all kids again in spirit.

As Little Richard screamed out "Good Golly, Miss Molly," Lainie grabbed Peter by the hand and pulled him into the guest bathroom. She locked the door behind them and started kissing him furtively, just like they'd kissed when they were seventeen. "Sshhh . . . be quiet . . . my mom . . . she's right outside the door . . ."

Peter immediately switched off the bright overhead light, leaving the soft glow from the art deco wall sconce, and like a teenager, he began feeling Lainie up underneath the sweater set. "Let's pet . . . just a little," he said, fumbling with her bra.

She turned around so that he could undo the bra and then leaned forward over the sink. She watched him in the mirror as his hands lifted her skirt and he began to touch her over her white cotton panties. He looked at her face reflected in the mirror as he held her hips and rubbed his crotch against her buttocks. "Let me put it in. Please. I won't come," he gasped, trying to remember all the things he used to say.

The noise outside the door increased as more people arrived, and Johnny Otis blared out over the speakers.

Suddenly someone pounded on the bathroom door. "Who's in there?" It was Lee.

"Nobody!" Peter sang out in a high "innocent" voice. Both he and Lainie burst out giggling.

"Jeeezzz . . ." growled Lee outside the door as he walked away. "They're making out in there. Where's the grown-ups around here anyway?"

For most of us, adolescence was a time of intense sexual awareness. The intensity was heightened further by the newness of the turf and the fact that it was forbidden. All this electrified the sex.

Take a foray back to those years to reignite those feelings.

After dusk, drive to a secluded place—preferably one with a view—replete with erotic memories. Cuddle, talk, and check out the scenery. Then take a step back into adolescence and pretend this is the first time you ever explored kissing and petting. Experiment with long and passionate kisses. Begin touching your partner over and then under clothing. But don't take anything completely off. Just spend an hour or so revisiting those early thrilling feelings.

◆

Rediscovering the past can revitalize a relationship, even one that is decades old.

◆

18. His and Her Night

♦ ♦ ♦ ♦ ♦ ♦ ♦ ♦ ♦ ♦ ♦ ♦ ♦ ♦ ♦

IT had never occurred to him that he could just lie back and enjoy sex. He didn't have to be the initiator. The doer. The guy, making it all work.

He had just spent a half hour stroking her lightly all over her body. She had taken his large hand in hers and showed him how she liked his fingertips to gently circle her nipples and trace little invisible electric lines down to her hips and inside her thighs. He had never known that about her. He loved watching her face as the delicate pleasure filled her. He was intrigued and moved to see the gooseflesh perk up her breasts and make her nipples stand straight out. All from such a gentle touch. And now it was his turn.

He guided her fingers to his nipples and then started rubbing them and pinching them roughly. She never would have thought of that. As he let go of her hand she seemed to slow down and get tender. That was okay, but he wanted it rough. He showed her again.

"This is how I like it," he whispered as he took his own nipples between his thumbs and index fingers and started vigorously kneading and pinching them. His pelvis undulated involuntarily, and his penis rose to half-mast.

She immediately took over and pressed and pinched and sucked and then nibbled his nipples. He loved it.

Then he dared to show her how he liked to touch his cock. He put her hand on it. She started massaging gently up and down.

"I like hard strokes. Guys aren't so dainty," he whispered, as he took it into his own hand and showed her. His cock was more than halfway hard . . . so he wrapped the palm of his hand around it and stroked vigorously. It was erect almost immediately.

"Let *me* do it," she said, with delight.

She took the wonderful plaything into her small

hand and vigorously stroked it up and down. He lay back on the pillow—nothing to do but enjoy. They had promised no intercourse here . . . just pleasuring each other. He closed his eyes and basked in the hot, sexy feelings as her hands stroked and kneaded and invented all kinds of new things to do with his cock. It made him glad to be a guy.

Set aside thirty to sixty minutes to enjoy each other sexually. The only activity that is off-limits is intercourse.

Decide who will be the giver and who will be the receiver.

The receiver's job is to receive and enjoy sexual pleasure.

- *Use verbal instructions.*
- *Guide your partner's hand by putting yours over it while using the kinds of strokes, rhythms, and pressures you prefer.*

- Demonstrate how you like your penis or clitoris touched.
- Take a risk and ask for things you may have never or only rarely tried before.
- Experiment. If an experiment proves disappointing, move on to something else.

The giver's role is to respond to his or her partner's wishes.

Provide your partner pleasure for a half hour, but do so in the ways your partner determines. After thirty minutes, switch roles. Or reverse roles on another occasion.

───────◆───────

The only rule is that you must say no to any activity or type of stimulation that you find very distasteful or unpleasant. Otherwise, try to expand your horizons by following your partner's lead.

───────◆───────

19. FOREPLAY

◆ ◆ ◆ ◆ ◆ ◆ ◆ ◆ ◆ ◆ ◆ ◆ ◆ ◆

The secret to great sex can be summed up in one word: foreplay.

Expand the time you usually spend on foreplay. Set aside a full hour to explore your partner's body. You might want to choose an early evening or a morning or afternoon when you have plenty of time.

Make a main course out of appetizers.

◆ *kissing*
◆ *massage*
◆ *oral sex*

Since the object is to prolong foreplay, the only activity that is off-limits is intercourse.

Touch, taste, and fully experience every part of your partner's body. Share fantasies if you like. The purpose of this activity is to heighten arousal, so relax and enjoy this time together. Fully appreciate the pleasure that extended foreplay provides.

———◆———

Foreplay is about "play." Here, the process is the purpose. The journey is more important than the destination.

———◆———

20. THE LAST TABOO

♦ ♦ ♦ ♦ ♦ ♦ ♦ ♦ ♦ ♦ ♦ ♦ ♦ ♦ ♦

SHE had never watched a man play with himself before. But here she was, leaning back against the pillows on the large bed and watching him fondle himself. She spread her legs and gently let her own fingers travel to the wet place between her legs.

He slowly stroked his balls. And then he took the base of his penis in his hand and gently slapped his soft cock against his left thigh; his cock started to grow. He closed his fingers gently around it and stroked up and down. She watched, mesmerized. She was almost unaware that her own fingers were exploring her clit, engorged and wet with desire. She slipped her fingers inside herself and pulled them out dripping with love juice. They slid back and forth against the bud that flourished between the soft folds of her inner lips.

Watching her, his cock got suddenly hard. He whimpered as a drop of milky white substance leaked out of the domed head.

She glanced up at his face, suddenly realizing that she had been totally focused on his penis and the way it responded to his touch. His eyes were watching her fingers play between her legs. The intensity of his gaze caused her to gasp. Then she slid her fingers deep inside again and again and began to make love to herself in earnest. She felt like a flower blooming in front of this man she had thought she knew so well.

Masturbation is one of the last taboos. But sharing this deeply personal aspect of your sexuality will not only teach each of you about your partner's sexual preferences, it can also deepen your sexual relationship. Increase your level of intimacy and your partner's knowledge of your sexuality by masturbating together.

First get into an erotic frame of mind. The follow-ing may help:

◆ *Describe a past sexual encounter.*
◆ *Make up a fantasy of your own.*
◆ *Read an erotic book aloud.*
◆ *View sensual photographs.*
◆ *Watch an erotic video.*
◆ *Light candles or incense.*
◆ *Kiss and touch your partner as usual.*

Once you have become aroused, begin to touch yourself. Stroke the different parts of your body in ways that you enjoy. Use an oil or some other lubri-cant to enhance your pleasure. Watch your partner as you stimulate yourself until each of you reaches orgasm.

———————◆———————

Notice if your partner's arousal enhances your own pleasure.

———————◆———————

STEP OUT AND TRY SOMETHING NEW

21. Sexual Innovation

◆ ◆ ◆ ◆ ◆ ◆ ◆ ◆ ◆ ◆ ◆ ◆ ◆ ◆ ◆

This was Alison's night to plan their lovemaking. She got home early and prepared a simple meal that would look effortlessly elegant—cracked crab, salad, and French bread. A half hour before Steve was due home, she set the table with flowers and candles. Frank Sinatra crooned on the stereo. When she heard Steve's car pull into the driveway she hurried to the front door and opened it just as he put his key in the lock.

Alison leaned against the doorjamb and smiled at Steve's reaction; she was wearing a new silk jersey dress that clung in all the right places. Before he could respond she said in a thick accent, "My name eez Genevieve. Alison couldn't be here tonight, so she has sent me to give you pleasure."

Steve felt a little awkward at first, but he was definitely interested. Alison/Genevieve invited him in, took off his jacket, and helped him undo his tie. She offered him wine in a crystal glass, and after they both took a sip, she asked him to dance. They danced in the living room near the open patio, where the decorated dinner table awaited them.

As the song ended, she moved him to the table. A small book tied in a silver ribbon rested on his plate. A rose lay on top. He picked up the book with interest. "Open eet," she said as she retreated to the kitchen. When she returned with the salads he was absorbed in the volume. She set the plates down, sat opposite him, and said, "Read eet aloud."

He blanched; it was almost as though the words stuck in his throat. She leaned in, put her chin on her hand, and dropped her eyelids a bit. "Pleeze, read eet to me . . ."

And he read: "His hand reached between her thighs, where his fingers could explore the smooth skin. As they traveled up and found the wetness between her legs, her eyes met his. He gently probed and stroked the pulsating bud that was hidden in the folds of her most private place."

Steve looked up at Alison with that musky look she loved so well. She gazed back and smiled. "Go on."

He did. "And as he moved his fingers back and forth, her eyes closed and her lips parted. She moaned with pleasure. Then she reached down and rested her hand over his and held his fingers inside her. When she was sure he would not pull them away, she moved her hand under his so that she could squeeze . . ."

Steve drifted off and couldn't continue. Alison reached for the book and then read in Genevieve's low, melodious voice, " . . . She moved her hand under his so that she could squeeze the bulging little bud with her fingers as he stroked in and out, in and out. Her head leaned back as she abandoned herself to pleasuring. He looked down at his large hand inside her and her smaller hand deftly bringing herself to the brink of orgasm and was stunned by the beauty of it. It was as though time stood still. 'Darling . . . I'm coming . . .' she cried. 'I'm coming all over you. See what you do to me. . . .' He could feel the electric current pour through his hand as she came . . ."

Alison and Steve gazed at each other for a long time before she gently closed the little volume and set it between the silver salt and pepper shakers. "We weel read more later. Pleeze, enjoy your meal. . . ."

Take a risk. Try something new when you make love.

◆ *Kiss your lover somewhere you never have before— on the fingertips or inner thighs.*
◆ *Try a prop—from satin sheets to sex toys. Buy something at a local sexual accoutrement store or from a mail-order catalog like the ones from Good Vibrations (800-289-8423) or Eve's Garden (800-848-3837).*
◆ *Read to each other from a book of erotica.*

- ◆ *Tongue your partner's ear, inside and out.*
- ◆ *Restrain your partner's arms by holding them firmly against the mattress.*

Love and intimacy can grow stale when taken for granted. Innovation is its own reward. Even the best gourmet dinner can get boring if it's served night after night.

———◆———

Lovemaking is like the sunset: every day the sun goes down, but every sunset is different.

———◆———

22. SEXUAL BREAKOUTS

◆ ◆ ◆ ◆ ◆ ◆ ◆ ◆ ◆ ◆ ◆ ◆ ◆ ◆

Break out of the routine by taking the opportunity to initiate sex in a new and different way.

◆ *Wake your partner in the middle of the night with a sexual caress.*

◆ *Make a secret plan for the children to spend the night with their grandparents or a special friend. Then seduce your partner.*

◆ *Leave a sexual invitation on your partner's personal voice mail or E-mail an erotic invitation to your partner at work.*

◆ *Create the perfect sexual environment, then blindfold your partner and lead him or her into it.*

◆ *Greet your partner at the door naked.*

A little originality goes a long way in creating great sex.

Because fear of rejection is so common, initiating sex may make you feel especially vulnerable. However, feeling vulnerable can lead to greater intimacy when a partner responds with loving acceptance.

23. RUTLESS RUTTING

◆ ◆ ◆ ◆ ◆ ◆ ◆ ◆ ◆ ◆ ◆ ◆ ◆ ◆

CARRIE was in mid-sentence when Taylor took her by the hand and turned her toward him. She had been gardening all morning and was saying something about the shed and potting soil and vitamin B for plants when he lifted her by the waist onto the patio table. Her skirt, which buttoned down the front, fell open to where it was undone just above the knees.

His right hand went directly for the sweet spot between her legs. Carrie tensed with surprise, then quickly began to relax as his knowing fingers played inside the soft folds.

He pressed her back onto the table and quickly unbuttoned the rest of her skirt with his free hand. She felt a surge of pleasure as his lips kissed down her tummy to the tuft of hair between her legs. His tongue searched between the folds to find the soft, throbbing bud he knew so well. When he touched it he felt the current of desire go through him like an electric shock. He loved this tender part of her. He kissed and licked and sucked her out there on the patio, under the sky, in front of God and the trees and flowers, until she ached to have him inside her.

Then he dropped his pants to his ankles, bent his knees slightly, and entered her slowly.

One way to add variety to your lovemaking is to try different intercourse positions. The Kama Sutra, The Joy of Sex, and other books detail many of them. Here are but a few ideas:

◆ *On your sides, the man's front pressed against the woman's back, spoon fashion.*
◆ *Rear entry—bent over the bathroom sink, kitchen counter, or office desk, or kneeling on the floor with the woman resting her upper body on a bed or sofa.*
◆ *Standing—while leaning against a wall for support.*

- Missionary position with the woman's knees pulled back toward her head.
- Woman on top with the man on his back, her legs between or outside his.
- Woman sitting on the man's lap facing toward him or away from him while he sits on a chair or the edge of a bed.
- Manually, stroke the woman's clitoris or cup the man's scrotum in a variety of intercourse positions.

Some positions won't work and others will be more humorous than arousing, but the novelty itself may prove exciting. Branch out and experiment with an innovative intercourse position. You may discover something new to add to your sexual repertoire.

———————◆———————

Sometimes subtle changes in a familiar position can add a touch of novelty.

———————◆———————

VEILING AND UNVEILING THE BODY FOR LOVEMAKING

24. Sexy Undergarments

♦ ♦ ♦ ♦ ♦ ♦ ♦ ♦ ♦ ♦ ♦ ♦ ♦ ♦

HE arrived with an old-fashioned Valentine's Day gift—a large heart-shaped box of candy with lace and frills on top. She opened the box, took a piece of dark chocolate, and placed it sensually between her lips. "I'll show this old-fashioned guy a new-fashioned thing or two," she thought as she eyed him demurely.

At that moment he pulled another gift from behind his back and extended it to her. It was wrapped in lacy paper with pink satin ribbon. Surprised, she set down the candy and examined the package. What could it be? He watched her with a curious sparkle in his eye; maybe this guy wasn't so square after all.

She carefully undid the delicate package to reveal a creamy white satin-and-lace teddy. She held it up to her body and looked at him. His eyes filled with desire, but he didn't move. He just stood there admiring her.

A surge of heat rushed through her; she'd had no idea this man was so sexy.

"Why don't you try it on," he said, "with high heels."

She blushed. He smiled warmly and continued to gaze at her. "I love you in high heels."

She was a little self-conscious but definitely inspired. By the time she returned to the living room he was sitting in the big chair, drinking a glass of wine. Her dress was unbuttoned over the teddy; her legs felt long and shapely in the high heels. She leaned against the wall, and the dress fell open as she looked at him across the room.

He set the glass of wine on the table next to him and leaned back to enjoy the visual feast. It was as though lightning bolts of sex emanated from his eyes and into the center of her being. She had never felt anything like it before.

"I want you to get wet just looking at me," he said

and smiled a smile so filled with warmth and sex that it completely disarmed her.

"What?" she asked, dazed.

As he repeated himself, she felt his maleness embrace her like a warm cloak and seep deep into her pores. It made her feel sexy, adored, and very female. She relaxed against the wall and let her dress fall casually off one shoulder. Her nipples were hard under the silky fabric of the teddy—it felt so good next to her skin. She let the dress fall completely off her shoulders and then leaned forward and pressed her breasts together with her arms. They looked even fuller than they were. He sighed audibly. She let the dress fall to the floor at her feet and dared to say what she had wanted to say all along: "And I want you to get hard just looking at me . . ."

To spice up your lovemaking, surprise your partner with a sexy piece of underclothing. Lingerie does not have to be expensive or only for women. There are lovely sensual teddies or nightgowns for women and silk undershorts in rich deep colors for men. Buy something sexy for your partner and wrap it attractively. Then casually present it shortly before you would like to make love. Asking your partner to model the gift can provide the perfect overture to a great encounter.

———————◆———————

Being touched through silky fabric can intensify sensual feelings.

———————◆———————

25. THE ART OF UNDRESSING

The art of undressing can become forgotten once a couple begins to share the same bed on a regular basis.

To bring back those intense early-courtship feelings, begin making love when you are still out of bed and dressed. Start in the living room or in the kitchen. Don't begin to remove each other's clothes until you reach high levels of arousal. Then you can take the clothing off slowly and seductively—one piece at a time—or you can passionately rip it off. Use the act of undressing to further heat up your lovemaking.

◆

One woman keeps tattered old clothes around just for this purpose. She and her partner dress in the old garb when they feel like literally ripping the clothing off one another.

◆

26. THE STRIPTEASE ◆ ◆ ◆ ◆ ◆ ◆ ◆ ◆ ◆ ◆ ◆ ◆

DON was jazzed. "Just feel sexy," he repeated to himself over and over like a mantra. "Feeling really sexy can make up for a multitude of mistakes," he thought as he blindfolded Laura with a silk scarf. He sat her in a comfortable chair, then fed her chocolates with his fingers. The champagne gave them both a buzz.

Then he dimmed the lights and turned up the music. As a lone sax wailed out into the room, he pulled the scarf gently away from Laura's eyes. Last month, when she had shyly mentioned she would love to see him do a striptease, she had no idea what she was in for.

He wore a trench coat and a fedora that made him look like a tough, 1930s gumshoe detective. He saw the delight fill her eyes, and his confidence soared. He turned, tilted his hat, and did a fancy step as the rhythm section started up and the brass lit into a hot rendition of "Honeysuckle Rose." "Honey, suck *my* rose," he said to himself as he swung his hips slowly to the music.

He turned his back to her, flashing the coat open and closed, then turning to face her again. The music was really turning him on.

The saxophone wailed and rasped as he pulled the trench coat off and threw it to the floor. He stood there in a tank T-shirt and silk boxer shorts with the fedora tilted over his right eye. He slowly pulled the silk shorts down to reveal a bit of pubic hair. His cock was hard. That's when the thought struck him: he was a private dick.

He laughed to himself as he turned and mooned her briefly. "Just a tease, ma'am, just a tease," he thought, feeling like Humphrey Bogart on a fucking good day. The trumpets caressed the sax up the scale. He pulled his shorts back and forth lightly over his cock.

He faced her and quickly pulled the shorts down, giving her a fleeting glimpse of his masterpiece. God that felt good!

All in all, he danced for about ten minutes. Saxes wailed, trumpets blared, and funky trombones seemed to pour the music right into his veins. He finally took his shorts off as he stood with his back to her. Then he took off his hat, covered his dick with it, and turned around to dance some more. He rested his hat on his hard cock. It stayed. Jeezus, this was fun.

He continued to look her in the eye as he danced. She was feeling hot—her eyes had that look in them. He pulled the hat away; his cock stood out as hard as a rock. He put the hat back over it and moved in closer to her. When he was standing right next to her, he pulled the hat away and tossed it to the floor. His cock pointed at her like a gun. He reached out for her hand, inviting her to dance.

She stood up and intentionally leaned forward to brush her cheek against his penis. She opened her robe as she rose and let his penis stroke down her bare torso and come to rest at the patch of hair where her legs joined. He didn't move his eyes from hers. "So, gorgeous, wouldja like ta dance?"

She answered, like the tough dame she had always wanted to be, "I'd like a little lap dancing, big guy, if the one-eyed snake is up for it."

"Yo, babe," he said. "The lap lizard is happy tonight."

He deftly spun her around, sat down in the chair and pulled her toward him. Her robe fell away as she straddled his legs and rested the soft lips of her cunt on the tip of his penis. She slowly moved it back and forth. He held her waist with his hands while she reached down to her pussy and spread it open for the one-eyed snake to rest its happy head. She moved slowly to the music, then gently lowered herself onto him.

The music throbbed in steady rhythm and rocked them like a ship on the ocean. They melted deeper and deeper into each other until his cock seemed to penetrate her soul. The sensation was exquisite.

Suddenly she came. Like a gusher. The big one. She cried, threw her arms around him and held on for dear life as he thrust himself up inside her again and again. "It feels like magic," he thought. "Her hot cunt feels like magic."

Then it was as though lightning struck. Right out the end of his cock. And they both seemed to light up in a blaze of fireworks. Jeezus fucking Christ! He closed his eyes and saw colored lights exploding inside his head. Then he felt himself dissolve right into her until there was nothing left of either of them . . . just music and the Fourth of July.

It went on and on until they came to rest on the shores of love. God, it was great to be a private dick.

Short, tall, big, small—bodies are wonderful in their infinite variety. Exposing your body and playing it as a fine instrument to arouse your partner can add exciting fun to your lovemaking. Creating an exotic striptease is a great way to do this.

Get dressed in something sexy. Turn the music up and the lights down. Gather a few scarves and pretend you're on the stage of a personal strip show. Seat your partner comfortably in a chair or on the bed.

Get into the mood by dancing seductively to the music. As you slowly remove your clothing—item by item—keep your eyes riveted on your partner. Drape the scarves across your semiclothed body and brush sensuously against your partner. Throw your inhibitions to the wind—this is the time for seductive play. Both men and women can do fabulous stripteases once they get into the mood.

Remember, no one views your body as critically as you are apt to do. The aspects of your body that turn your partner on are more than likely different from the qualities sought by magazine editors and marketing experts. Now is the time to make your partner's preferences count.

———————◆———————

The style of the music—Middle Eastern, rock, jazz, romantic, classical—can dramatically influence the experience.

———————◆———————

BROADENING THE SEXUAL BOUNDARIES

27. Sex al Fresco

◆ ◆ ◆ ◆ ◆ ◆ ◆ ◆ ◆ ◆ ◆ ◆ ◆ ◆

THEY walked for over an hour across sandy alcoves and around rock jetties that protruded out into the surf. Fred shouldered the picnic basket and Diana carried the blanket and towels. The air smelled fresh and salty, filling them with a sense of well-being.

A wave receded, giving them just enough room in the wet sand to round another rocky cliff. As soon as she saw what lay ahead, Diana knew they had found the perfect place. The beach was secluded, the sand was dry, the dunes went straight up, and they hadn't seen another person for miles. She ran toward the dry sand as a new wave rolled in and crashed against the rocks. Fred followed her, laughing.

Diana spread out the large blanket and quickly removed all her clothes. As Fred set the picnic basket down she danced around happily, naked, feeling free and ecstatic. Fred, cautious as always, looked around to make sure nobody was watching. When he was satisfied that they were alone, he quickly dropped his shorts onto the blanket. Diana turned to look at him. Here they were, both nude on the wide-open beach, under the sky. She walked toward him and stopped with her breasts lightly touching his chest. She felt his penis begin to awaken near the soft patch of her pubic hair.

She inhaled freedom along with the salt and sunshine and fresh air, then slowly let her body begin to move against his in a sultry dance. Liquid, languid, and spontaneous.

His cock was soon very hard. Diana knelt in front of him on the blanket and wrapped her lips around it. Her tongue took on a life of its own as it danced and flicked and sucked the smooth contours of his penis.

They made love for hours. It was as though the crashing waves filled them with a kinetic force that vitalized every cell in their bodies and carried them both to its own powerful conclusion. Again and again and again.

Making love outdoors can be remarkable, especially when there may be a slight chance of being caught.

Take two large beach towels and hike to a secluded beach or wooded area (where there are no people, poison oak, or poison ivy).

Lie on one beach towel; even if no one is likely to pass by, you may want to place the second discreetly over you.

Allow the beauty of nature to inspire your lovemaking.

———————◆———————

There is nothing like the outdoors to awaken your instincts.

———————◆———————

28. HOT, WET SEX

◆ ◆ ◆ ◆ ◆ ◆ ◆ ◆ ◆ ◆ ◆ ◆

For fun, allow a hot bath to provide the setting for a passionate lovemaking scene. Draw the bathwater and then pour in some luxurious bubble bath. Floating candles can add a romantic touch.

Or consider a hot tub (sans bubble bath, of course). Many spas provide private rooms.

Once the bath is prepared, step into the hot water with your partner and relax. Breathe deeply and exhale the stress and worry from your body. As the heat of the water warms you from the outside, soft stroking and tender words can warm you from the inside.

Then, as the water begins to cool, step out of the tub and seductively towel each other dry. The bed or a rug in front of a fireplace may be appropriate places to continue the action.

---◆---

This is one example of how a simple, everyday event can be easily transformed into a sensual, intimate, and romantic moment.

---◆---

29. TREASURE HUNT

◆ ◆ ◆ ◆ ◆ ◆ ◆ ◆ ◆ ◆ ◆ ◆ ◆ ◆

BRENT was finishing a phone call when his secretary entered with a pastry box from Mani's, the health bakery.

"It's from your wife. Isn't she still in Chicago?"

"She'll be home day after tomorrow," he said as he reached for the box.

She stood and watched as he opened it to reveal a small chocolate forest cake, his favorite. He opened the attached card and grinned as he read:

To find yourself in a daze of delight,
Check the drawer by your bedside tonight.
                                        —*Elana*

Of course, the first thing Brent did when he got home was hurry upstairs to his bedside table. Inside was a wooden box tied with a white ribbon. How had she put it there without his noticing? He pulled off the ribbon and opened the box to find a marked-up map and this note:

Find your way here by seven P.M.
   the day before I come home, and then
I guarantee that you will find
   at the end of your journey a wonderful time.

It wasn't hard for him to find the spot, as they had hiked Muir Woods many times before. As familiar as he was with the terrain, he couldn't anticipate what to expect and kept scanning the greenery around him. He rounded the bend to the last clearing and there it was: Elana herself sitting on a large, plaid blanket with a full-course meal spread out in front of her. A chilled bottle of champagne sat in a silver bucket; a warm smile danced on her face. "Happy just-for-the-fun-of-it, hon," she said.

The treasure hunt is a terrific way to lead your partner to a birthday present, anniversary gift, marriage proposal, or plain old seduction.

Begin with a written note or a message on your partner's voice mail or answering machine with the first clue. Then, by prearranging the steps, leave cards and clues, each one leading to the next, until you end up at the final destination.

◆ *Attach a note to a rose waiting in a florist's shop.*
◆ *Wrap a note in a box with one truffle to be picked up at a local candy store.*
◆ *Place a clue inside the refrigerator, beneath a lily in the garden, or under your partner's pillow.*

The special surprise that awaits your partner at the end could be anything from a new CD to an engagement ring.

Or the final destination itself could be the surprise—maybe a room in a quaint hotel or inn.

———————◆———————

Even the most modest gift becomes exceptional when the presentation is done artfully.

———————◆———————

USING SEX TO TOUCH SOULS

30. MAKING LOVE

◆ ◆ ◆ ◆ ◆ ◆ ◆ ◆ ◆ ◆ ◆ ◆ ◆

THE words hung in his mind all day: "We never make love anymore." He had heard that it happened to other couples, but he had never thought it would happen to them.

He spent the afternoon almost in a panic, wondering what to do about it. Was this the way they were going to spend the rest of their lives—too busy to connect and too embarrassed to talk about it? Were they just too far away from the tender part of their loving to ever need each other the way they used to? At this rate they were going to end up like their parents—polite and bored and withholding. Is that what he wanted?

"No. I don't think so," he thought. "Love has to start somewhere. Why not with me?"

He finished shaving and looked at himself in the mirror. It had been a while since he had shaved before going to bed. He buttoned the silk pajamas he had purchased on his lunch hour. His heart was actually pounding. Was he excited or nervous? He wasn't sure, but he sure as hell wasn't going to let it stop him.

As he entered the bedroom he stood in the doorway to look at her. She sat with pillows propped behind her, focusing on her laptop computer, which sat on the breakfast tray in front of her. Funny. He had never noticed how adorable she was in those half glasses. And that T-shirt. He stood in the doorway and gazed at her, unsure what to do next. Should he interrupt? Would she laugh at his romantic overtures? Should he turn back now before she noticed him in those silly pajamas?

She glanced up briefly, then did a double take. "Too late," he thought and froze; he felt vulnerable to the core.

She took off her glasses and looked at him quizzically. He couldn't think of anything glib to say as he crossed the room toward her, so he just said, "Hi, honey. Whatcha doing?"

Much to his relief, she patted the bed beside her and replied, "Nothing much. Come sit down."

He sat. Neither of them knew what to say next, so he took the plunge and tried to say what was in his heart.

"So . . . I was thinking . . . about what you said. And how we are . . . and . . . I . . . ah. . . ." The words seemed to stick in his throat. "Well . . . I would really like to try it."

She wasn't quite sure what he was talking about, or else she couldn't believe her ears. "It?"

"Yeah . . . you know. I'd really like us to . . . you know . . . be like we were. I mean . . ."

He stopped and looked at her in a kind of anguish. He hoped against hope that she would help him out as she always did.

And she did.

"Did you shave?" she asked shyly. He nodded. "For me?" He nodded again.

Her face lit up like a Christmas tree. She looked unabashedly happy; their years together seemed to melt away in the light of that smile, and they were both young and tender again. She suddenly became self-conscious of her T-shirt.

He brushed a strand of hair away from her face. "I love you, you know. And I just want to . . . not get us lost . . . in the shuffle."

And that night they looked into each other's eyes as they made love. They noticed each other's bodies again, and the richness and ripeness of their feelings for each other. They discovered that the bond of knowing each other so well had created a bridge of gratitude and appreciation that became the most profound kind of lovemaking.

You can "have sex" and you can "make love." They are not necessarily the same thing. When you "make love," you open yourself completely to your mate. As you let go and allow your body to follow its own instincts, stay in touch with your heart and your loving feelings for your partner.

There are many ways to do this:

◆ Think about how much you love your partner.
◆ Tell your partner that you love him or her.
◆ Adore your partner's body as you make love to it.
◆ Hold each other and breathe together.
◆ Look lovingly into your partner's eyes.

Make love and allow yourself completely to feel the love you have for your mate.

———————◆———————

Making love "from the heart" can create the deepest and most profound sex.

———————◆———————

31. Staying on the Edge

◆ ◆ ◆ ◆ ◆ ◆ ◆ ◆ ◆ ◆ ◆ ◆ ◆ ◆

LILA loved feeling the head of his cock rub against her clit. He could bring her to orgasm with that alone. The sweet, smooth rod moved back and forth inside her. Just before she went over the falls, she held her breath and put her fingers on his cock to let him know to stop. They wanted the lovemaking to last.

She took a deep breath and let her energy subside. She could feel the excitement rushing through her veins. As soon as she knew she wasn't going to come, she started kissing him—deep, sexy, lingering kisses. His cock grew hard again in the wet folds of her pussy.

She felt him move the head of his penis very slowly in and out of the magic doorway. Again and again. It was as though he was gently opening her and filling her with hot love. When he was close to orgasm, he stopped and held his position inside her. Finally he pulled out and balanced back on his knees, looking down at her; his cock stuck out from his body—hard, wet, and quivering. He waited a moment, then closed his eyes; he didn't want the sight of her to stimulate him any more just then. When the intensity of his feeling subsided, he opened his eyes. She lay there like a luscious fantasy waiting for him to get lost in her.

His hands roamed down to the love place where his cock had just been. His fingers entered her. She was still wet and hot. His fingers curled up inside her vagina to touch the magic spot on the front wall. It felt energized and alive, the tissue was engorged with excitement. He stroked it with his finger, slowly, slowly, again and again. She moaned and groaned and felt as though she was losing consciousness. "*Le Petit Mort*. This is what the French mean by 'the little death,' " she thought.

They continued like this for well over an hour. Changing positions, changing techniques, stopping just at the edge of orgasm to let the energy subside, then building it up again.

When they finally allowed themselves to come, all the accumulated intensity came rushing forth. All they could do was hold on to each other and cry out.

Their orgasms went on for what seemed like a long time—pure ecstasy shooting through their systems like adrenaline. And when it was finally over they found themselves in each other's arms, melted into a puddle of sublime happiness.

The longer sexual excitement is maintained, the more intense the orgasm is likely to be. To intensify the sexual release, try to stay at a high level of arousal for as long as possible before cresting to orgasm.

Make love until you feel you are getting close to orgasm. Then:

- *Stop the stimulation for a few seconds.*
- *Slow down.*

- ◆ Lighten the touch.
- ◆ Tense your pelvic or buttock muscles.
- ◆ Change positions.
- ◆ Do something else that will briefly lower your level of arousal.

You will need to let your partner know when to back off and when to resume stimulation. This can be done verbally or through body language (backing away, pressing forward).

See how long you can remain on the edge of orgasm without spilling over.

———————◆———————

This is one of the places we can linger in life . . . and not feel guilty.

———————◆———————

32. Soul Gazing

◆ ◆ ◆ ◆ ◆ ◆ ◆ ◆ ◆ ◆ ◆ ◆ ◆ ◆

Looking deeply into your partner's eyes at the point of high arousal and orgasm can connect you together more profoundly both physically and spiritually. But don't try this until you are fairly comfortable with prolonging arousal and are able to hang out on the plateau preceding orgasm for at least a couple of minutes.

To begin, stimulate each other manually, orally, or in any way that brings you to a high level of arousal. Then assume a position where you can look into each other's eyes while you each manually stimulate your own or your partner's genitals. Continue this for a few minutes or for as long as possible before experiencing orgasm.

The eyes are the windows to the soul. Here is one of the places where sexuality and spirituality converge.

33. The Blending of Sex and Soul

♦ ♦ ♦ ♦ ♦ ♦ ♦ ♦ ♦ ♦ ♦ ♦ ♦

HE entered her from on top. They gazed into each other's eyes as he slowly pressed himself inside her. He watched her face soften as the glow of pleasure spread over her. He had never looked directly into her eyes as they made love before; he had never known how deeply he affected her.

He saw her struggle to keep her eyes from closing so as not to disconnect from his gaze. He pumped slowly and felt the intense feelings overwhelm her again. It was as though he was looking deep into her core—and all he could see was love and sex and pulsing aliveness responding to his smallest move.

His cock felt strong and hot inside her. It bulged involuntarily with a throbbing force. He winced with pleasure but never looked away from her eyes. "She must be seeing the same thing in me," he thought. He pumped deeper, now trying to penetrate her heart and soul. Then suddenly it happened—an explosion of energy ignited between them. Their eyes, their hearts, their genitals . . . everything seemed to melt together in a brilliant flash of ecstasy.

He cried out as he collapsed down to orgasm with her. It was as though they were spinning out into space together. He clung to her. The ripples of her orgasm resonated through his body as if their two separate beings had melted into one.

Gaze into each other's eyes, but this time, do it while having intercourse. This can be done with the man on top, with the woman on top, or while you are in a sitting or even a standing position—any position where you are face-to-face. The woman may want additional manual clitoral stimulation to help her maintain her level of arousal during intercourse. Linger at levels of high arousal for as long as possible, continuing to gaze into each other's eyes—even through orgasm.

———————◆———————

Lovemaking can grow more ecstatic month after month and year after year. There is virtually no limit to the possibilities of soulful sexuality.

———————◆———————

WHO SAYS YOU HAVE TO BE IN THE SAME PLACE TO ENJOY SEX?

34. DEPARTURES

◆ ◆ ◆ ◆ ◆ ◆ ◆ ◆ ◆ ◆ ◆ ◆ ◆ ◆ ◆

BILL handed the bellman a tip, then threw his overnighter on the bed. He hated these trips, the same sterile hotel rooms and the same overpriced hotel food. Perhaps he could find a nice cozy little restaurant somewhere, he thought, as he opened his suitcase. The prospect of hunting for one didn't thrill him; jet lag and the thought of tomorrow's meetings made him long for some homemade soup and his comfortable bed.

Bill lifted his suit out of the case and something fell to the floor. He reached for it.

Black lace panties.

As he picked them up, a note tied with a red satin ribbon dangled delicately in the air. He hurriedly hung up his suit and sat on the bed to read the note. He couldn't help but grin.

Hurry home, darling.
I love you and want you and need you . . .
Inside me.

He held the delicate panties to his face and inhaled deeply; the fragrance of her perfume filled his senses.

Before one of you goes out of town on a trip, spend a few minutes planting the seeds of desire for the return home.

Surreptitiously place a loving note, a silly or suggestive card, or even one of your sexiest undergarments in the departing partner's suitcase—or in the refrigerator, underwear drawer, or beneath the pillow of the partner remaining home. Describe what you plan to do to your partner sexually upon reuniting.

Then act on it when the traveling partner returns.

Some people write a brief erotic story to keep a partner entertained while they are separated—a good way to keep the home fires burning.

35. Phone Sex

❖❖❖❖❖❖❖❖❖❖❖❖❖❖

THE delivery person handed her a package wrapped in brown paper and asked her to sign for it. She did so with a flourish, pretending it was vitamins or a reader's light from a mail-order catalog.

She glanced at the return address: "Good Vibes, San Francisco." The deliveryman didn't seem to know or care what Good Vibes was. She made a comment about wind chimes, handed him back his pen, and closed the door.

She ran up the stairs two at a time, tearing open the package. She hurried to her bedroom and finished opening it on her bed. A dildo. Shaped like a large, pink penis. She quickly pulled two AA batteries out of her drawer.

As she waited for the phone to ring, she reclined on her bed against a mound of pillows. She felt luxurious and somewhat decadent—not only was she lying in bed in the middle of the afternoon, she was masturbating. Without guilt. Wide open for all the pictures on the wall to see. Her only regret was that she didn't have a mirror on the ceiling.

The phone rang at three on the dot; he was always on time. The eight-hour time difference put him at eleven P.M. She lifted the phone and said "Hello." Her voice was husky.

"Honey? Is that you," said Kit, on the other end of the line. He sounded like he was across town, not across an ocean in London.

"Yes . . . it's me. . . ." It felt so erotic to be talking to him on the phone while working the smooth, vibrating little head in and out of her vagina.

"Are you okay?" He sounded concerned.

"Uh-huh . . . I got it. It's wonderful."

His voice changed immediately. "It is? Are you using it now?"

"Uh-huh . . . I'm lying on the bed without any clothes on massaging myself with it."

"Tell me about it. . . ." He lay back on his bed, unzipped his fly, and reached for his penis. He gently started stroking himself as they spoke.

She was getting more and more excited. "Well, I'm pushing the end of it in and out of my cunt. And now I'm letting it slide around my clit . . . oh, God. . . . It feels so good, honey . . ."

"I've got my cock in my hand. It's hard. Just thinking about you. I want to put it inside you . . ."

She thrust the dildo deep inside her and cried out as she arched back. "Oh . . . it's way inside me. Just like you. I feel your voice deep inside me . . . oh, talk to me, honey . . . just let me hear your voice while I come . . ."

"Come on, baby. I want to hear you come. . . ." He could hear the sounds she was making over the phone. The energy was palpable. He looked down at his cock and stroked it harder as she groaned and he talked. "I'm really hard, baby. I'm going to come with you . . . tell me when . . . okay, baby? I love to hear you come . . . I'm going to come with you, honey. Get that cock deep inside you, baby . . . feel me . . . come on, baby . . ."

"Oh . . ." she cried as she pulled the vibrating dildo out to stroke her clit again. "Oh . . . it's starting. . . ." She threw her head back and cried out, "I'm coming, honey . . . I'm coming." She thrust the dildo back inside her and rubbed its vibrating end against the magic spot on the front wall of her vagina. The mouth of her vagina contracted around the wonderful pink dildo. The vibrations were so intense that she had to turn the vibrator off. But her vagina continued to suck and pulse around that wonderful rubber cock even after it was quiet. Then she heard Kit. He cried out, "I love you, Chrissy . . . oh, Chrissy . . . oh . . . Chrissy . . . oh. . . ." He came and came. She lay back, closed her eyes, and absorbed every nuance of his voice.

Ahh . . . the telephone. . . . Reach out and touch someone.

When your partner is out of town, or when the two of you cannot be together for some reason, make love over the phone.

You can create a sexual fantasy, read to each other from an erotic book, or just describe aloud what you are doing to your own body as you stimulate yourself.

Giving voice to your orgasm can be the most exciting part of all.

———————◆———————

One woman I know dials her partner's answering machine when she knows he's not at home and immediately hangs up. Then she masturbates, and just as she is about to come, she hits redial and has her orgasm after she hears the sound of the beep. Needless to say, her lover always listens to his messages in private.

———————◆———————

PUSHING BEYOND SAFE BOUNDARIES

36. Obstacles as Catalysts

◆ ◆ ◆ ◆ ◆ ◆ ◆ ◆ ◆ ◆ ◆ ◆ ◆ ◆ ◆

THE grandparents had insisted they all go to Disneyland. It was only once a year that they saw their grandchildren, and they had every intention of spoiling them rotten.

It started while they were all standing in line for the Teacups. Jessica leaned back against Paul as they watched Gram and Gramps talking earnestly to the very excited twins. Those four were definitely having a wonderful time, but there were other things Jessie would rather be doing with Paul—they had so little time together as it was. Here they were, stuck in crowds all day with two seven-year-olds and her parents. Hmmm . . . she leaned back against his body and gently tucked her buttocks into his crotch. She wished that they were still in bed. To her delight, Paul leaned in toward her; his hips seemed to rest on her two cheeks, and his soft penis nestled in the crack. She looked around; had anyone noticed? No. There was so much excitement around that nobody was interested in two ordinary, middle-class people in a crowd.

The line moved forward, and their turn came; Gram and Gramps ran with the kids to the pink Teacup with white polka dots. Jessica and Paul didn't move from where they stood next to the railing. Jess waved to her parents as they beckoned for her to come onto the ride. Jessica shook her head and smiled. She was having a much nicer ride where she was. Paul's cock was getting hard against the crack of her rump. Oh, if her mom only knew. Jessica laughed out loud and waved to the excited kids as they spun by her, squealing. Paul put his arms around her and nestled his head down by her shoulder.

"I want to fuck you. Right here. Right now," he whispered, and then waved to the kids as they whirled around to the other side of the ride. Then he brought his arm across Jessica's chest, brushing his forearm against her breasts. Her nipples got hard under the little T-shirt. Uh-oh. She glanced around. This was Disneyland, for Christ's sake. He continued in his most sexy voice, "But I think I'm going to make love to you all day in my mind . . ."

As the day wore on, both grandparents and grandchildren had the time of their lives in the big playground for kids of all ages . . . while Paul and Jessica had the time of *their* lives playing the games that grown-ups play. All in all, it was a wonderful day filled with double entendres, subtle and not-so-subtle teasing, and the joy of longing for something that they both knew they were going to get. Paul and Jessica flirted on Main Street, sized each other up in Tomorrowland, and petted heavily on the Pirates of the Caribbean ride—and Paul got such a hard-on in Frontierland that they took another time around in the boat. Each obstacle heightened their sexual tension.

When they arrived home, neither could wait to get the other into bed.

Passion can be heightened by the tension created when you have to overcome certain impediments to making love. Think about your teenage years, when there was nothing but obstacles, and how encountering them intensified your sexual feelings.

Begin by going out with your partner and pretending that you cannot go back home to make love. Somehow, you have to figure out a way to enjoy each other sexually despite this impediment. Then do your best to creatively solve the challenge you've set up.

◆

When asked for their best sexual encounters, many people will recall experiences when they had to overcome some obstacle before they could consummate their sexual union.

◆

37. TRANSFORMING JEALOUSY

◆ ◆ ◆ ◆ ◆ ◆ ◆ ◆ ◆ ◆ ◆ ◆ ◆ ◆ ◆

Noticing that your lover is attractive to others can stimulate your own feelings of sexual desire, just as being desired by others can enhance your confidence as a sexual being.

Just before you leave to go to a social event with your partner, make an agreement that you both can innocently flirt with others to your heart's content—this entails animated conversation and, particularly, engaged eye contact. Provocative interchanges and innuendo are all fair game, but under no circumstances should either of you lead your acquaintances on.

Be sure to relegate equal time to flirting with your partner. Have fun and let the sexual juices flow.

Agree that if either of you begins to feel uncomfortably jealous, he or she will let the other person know, and agree to use the opportunity to depart and have a party of your own. Otherwise, wait until the end of the evening to take those flirtatious feelings home and transform them into fabulous lovemaking.

This is a great activity for people with "the grass is always greener" syndrome.

---

38. THE HIDDEN FORBIDDEN

◆ ◆ ◆ ◆ ◆ ◆ ◆ ◆ ◆ ◆ ◆ ◆ ◆

HE watched Tina's hips sway gently under the black jersey dress as the maître d' showed her to a table at the back of the restaurant. Will had specifically asked for the small table with a booth seat on the far side. He slipped in next to her; there was no way he was going to sit *across* from her when she was looking so sexy in that clingy dress.

As the waiter left to get their wine, Will let his hand slip under the long white tablecloth and opened the front of her wraparound skirt. The jersey felt rich and luxurious next to her skin. Her thighs were bare above the high-top nylons. He found it hard to pretend conversation as his fingers traveled up to her private place. She smiled like the Mona Lisa.

The waiter appeared, setting their wine in front of them and reciting the evening specials. Both Will and Tina looked up and listened politely, if a little glassy-eyed, while the waiter seemed to babble on forever with his long list of poached this and sautéed that. At last he got to the good part: "I'll just come back to take your order," he said as he turned to leave.

As the waiter walked away, Will felt Tina's hand reach over and cup his crotch. "Maybe *I'll* just *come* before he does," she whispered with a twinkle in her eye while she began to gently knead Will's cock.

Will glanced nervously around; no one was watching. The dimly lit room was designed for romance. It struck him that maybe the long white tablecloths were part of the plan.

He took a deep breath and helped Tina unzip his fly. As her agile fingers reached inside his pants and touched the tender head of his penis, he knew he was in for an amazing meal.

There is nothing more exciting than the forbidden. And what could be more forbidden than illicit fondling in public, when no one but the two of you knows what's going on?

◆ *Duck into the rest room in a restaurant—or on an airplane.*
◆ *Take advantage of a dark theater at an off hour.*
◆ *Bring a small lap blanket on a long bus trip.*

———————◆———————

Be careful while you have fun. There are laws against indecent exposure.

———————◆———————

ENHANCE YOUR LOVE-MAKING WITH WORDS AND IMAGES

39. EROTIC VIDEOS

◆ ◆ ◆ ◆ ◆ ◆ ◆ ◆ ◆ ◆ ◆ ◆ ◆

SHE was glad Tom was with her. She never would have had the nerve without him. She would have gazed vacantly at the aisles and aisles of videos lit up by those harsh fluorescent lights and ended up getting something the kids would enjoy. As it was, Tom headed directly to the back corner of the store while she dawdled in Romantic Comedy, then feigned interest in the Classics.

Just then a nice-looking man stepped out of the back room with two tapes under his arm. He headed straight for the front counter as she stared after him. He was clean-cut, well-dressed, and, well, he didn't look like a biker or anything.

"Pssstt! Karen!" whispered Tom from where he stood just inside the doorway.

Karen quickly but nonchalantly put the video box

she was holding back on the shelf and slipped into the den of iniquity.

Whew. She'd done it. She looked around and was amazed to see pictures of voluptuous women lasciviously offering their open legs and tender crotches to the world. Tall babes with big tits on boxes with words like "confidential" and "sexy screenings" printed in bold type. It frightened and fascinated her. And made her wet.

Tom pointed to a video cover of a woman in black leather with her nipples peeking through the cutouts of her black leather bra. Hmm. That looked a little over-the-top for tonight; maybe some other time. Karen reached for a box with a pretty woman in a white lace dress. It could have been a romance novel, except her bare nipples showed through the delicate lace and a small photo inset showed two men fucking her at the same time. A dead giveaway that this was not *Gone With the Wind*.

"I don't think I can make an intelligent choice," whispered Karen.

"I don't think intelligence is required," said Tom, laughing. "Just choose. If we pick a few, we'll have some options."

Another man walked in—nice-looking, unassuming. He hesitated when he saw Karen and turned away to study the opposite wall: cunts, cocks, tits, and butts seemed to leap out from their places on the shelves in a cacophony of sexual positions.

She quickly reached for two videos, showed them to Tom, who nodded, and then she pulled him out of there.

When they got home, Karen set up the bed with pillows and Tom brought in two glasses of Cabernet. She put on her lace peignoir and he wore his silk robe. *Click.* The first video started to roll. Beautiful bodies. Silly acting. Story ludicrous. But then the leading lady lay back on a chaise longue and began to masturbate. With his eyes on her, the leading man pulled his cock out of his pants and began to massage himself. Karen couldn't believe she was sitting there with Tom watching all this. It was both unnerving and exciting.

The leading man straddled the leading lady, and she sucked his cock until it got so long and hard that it arched up and quivered. The veins in the side bulged, and when a little white drop of come appeared, Karen and Tom both watched, intrigued.

Then the leading man pulled his giant cock away from the leading lady's mouth and kissed down her body all the way to her neatly trimmed pubic hair. He gently parted the folds of flesh so that the camera could clearly see her pink bud; the delicate flesh petals wrapped around it like an exotic flower. He put the head of his cock up to that little pink doorway and gently probed. Karen held her breath. She reached for Tom's leg and stroked the inside of his thigh. She could tell by the tension on the silk of his robe that he was getting hard.

The leading man then slipped his cock inside that secret of all secret places—the treasure trove that men have been fighting over since the beginning of time. Something primal seemed to leap off the screen and fill the room.

Karen and Tom didn't say a word . . . they just slowly slipped into a world of sensuous bodies and mindless play. Tom's touch felt electric on Karen's skin. His fingers felt juicy in her cunt. As they watched the couple on the screen make love, a charge of energy leaped out of the T.V. like a palpable current. Soon Tom was inside Karen and they were swept away on a wave of pure sex. The woman on the screen orgasmed; then the man pulled out his hard cock and spurted milky white come all over her belly. The intensity that blasted through Karen and Tom washed away everything else. Soon the celluloid couple were left far behind as Karen and Tom dove deeper and deeper into the pure joy that lives at the core of sex.

Rent an erotic film or patronize an adult movie theater. With a sense of fun, you can turn this experience into an erotic adventure.

Don't worry if the film doesn't turn you on. Even if you are not aroused or feel mildly amused, you may notice that it has the effect of making you more passionate or sexually creative.

Some good erotic videos:

HARD R-RATED VIDEOS
By Deborah Films:
Cabin Fever
The Voyeur
The Hottest Bid

X-RATED VIDEOS

By Femme Productions:
  Sensual Escape
  Urban Heat

Susie Bright's recommendations:
  Every Woman Has a Fantasy
  Autobiography of a Flea
  Only the Best, volume 1
  Only the Best, volume 2

———————◆———————

Watching erotic videos can also be a great way to get new sexual ideas.

———————◆———————

40. Erotic Literature

*Build your sexual energy. Look at a sexy magazin
with your partner or buy an erotic book that has
style you enjoy, and read aloud to your partn
before you begin making love (or even while you a
making love).*

Some good erotic literature:

By Nickelson Baker:
Vox
The Fermata

Edited by Lonnie Barbach:
Pleasures: Women Write Erotica
Erotic Interludes: Tales Told by Women
The Erotic Edge: Erotica for Couples

Edited by Susie Bright:
Herotica I, II, and III
The Best of American Erotica, 1993, 1994, and 1995

By Henry Miller:
Black Spring
Tropic of Cancer
Tropic of Capricorn

By Anaïs Nin:
Delta of Venus
Little Birds

———◆———

Erotica written by male writers can differ dramatically from erotica written by female writers. Experiment to learn your preferences.

———◆———

41. HOME VIDEOS

◆ ◆ ◆ ◆ ◆ ◆ ◆ ◆ ◆ ◆ ◆ ◆ ◆ ◆

PENNY had always wanted to do this . . . ever since seeing the eating scene in *Tom Jones*. Gil set the video camera on a tripod at the foot of the bed while she arranged the feast on the large bedspread. Finger food, wine, and more finger food . . . succulent, soft, gooey, crunchy . . . she had it all. When the stage was set, they helped each other into their "costumes"—softly draped fabric reminiscent of ancient Rome and *I, Claudius*. Perfect for an orgy—especially on videotape.

Penny lolled luxuriously on the bed while Gil started the camera. He zoomed in to get a focus, and she immediately set the mood . . . she took a large strawberry, put it sensually between her lips, and sucked before taking a bite. Then she looked straight into the camera and wet her fingers with the tip of her tongue and slowly spread the wetness around her lips.

Gil smiled from where he stood behind the lens. Penny moved her leg so that the makeshift toga fell open, revealing her soft inner thigh. Then she reached for a piece of chicken just as Gil slid onto the bed next to her. She sensually tore off a bite with her teeth and held the rest out for him. He moved close and let her feed him; then he sucked her fingers clean. As they continued to feed each other, Gil's penis grew tall and raised the fabric of his costume like a tent. Penny's top fell open to reveal her delicate small breasts and hard nipples.

They continued to feed and feel each other and to suck and drink and eat until Penny could no longer keep her mouth away from the pleasure of Gil's cock. And as she sucked and moaned he leaned back luxuriously while the camera continued to roll.

Many people who would otherwise enjoy X-rated videos complain that the actresses look bored sexu-

ally, that the acting is abysmal, or that the sexual violence is offensive. To counter these objections, film your own erotic video.

If you don't own a video camera, rent one. Set the camera on a tripod or on a dresser or chair and take aim. Turn up the lights. Call "Action" and start the camera.

♦ If you enjoy play-acting, create a script and cast yourself and your partner in the leading roles.
♦ If you feel performance pressure, begin under the covers and make love as usual.

When you feel so inclined, stop the action, rewind the tape, and view it as a way to whet your appetite for continuing further. Or wait and watch the tape as a prelude to the next time you make love.

♦

Be sure to erase the tape as soon as possible. Ever with the best precautions, these tapes have an uncanny way of falling into the wrong hands.

♦

TAKE A BREAK FROM REALITY AND HAVE SOME FUN

42. ACT OUT A FANTASY

◆ ◆ ◆ ◆ ◆ ◆ ◆ ◆ ◆ ◆ ◆ ◆ ◆ ◆ ◆

SUSAN saw Ollie's car as soon as she turned into the parking lot. She pulled into an open space near his, checked her hair and makeup, then got out and smoothed the hem of her miniskirt. She let her hips sway back and forth as she strutted through the front door and across the lobby. As she approached the front desk she saw her husband checking in. She pretended she didn't know him.

"Hello. A single room please," she announced to the desk clerk. "With a king-sized bed."

The clerk gave her papers to fill out. "I'm sorry," he said. "We have no more king-sized beds. But I have several rooms with double queens."

"Hmmm. . . ." Susan pouted with a little frown.

Ollie, wearing the slate-blue silk shirt Susan had given him for his birthday, leaned over and started to flirt.

"I got the last king-sized bed. But I'll share."

Susan looked at him askance and went back to filling out her papers. He moved in closer.

"You here alone?"

The clerk tried to interrupt. "Sir . . . we don't . . ."

"I can take care of myself, thank you," replied Susan firmly to the young man behind the desk. Then she looked up at Ollie and flirted outrageously. "I'm just here with me, myself, and I."

Ollie grinned. "A ménage à trois. Sounds like fun."

The clerk gasped and cleared his throat.

"So . . . ah . . . I just got in from New York," continued Ollie. "Where're *you* from?"

"Here. They are fumigating my house for termites. I need to stay away for three days."

"Oh . . . so, you must know a great place to eat."

"Lots of them."

She stopped filling out the forms and eyed Ollie up

and down seductively. The clerk gawked as the sexual energy crackled between them.

Then Ollie did the kind of thing she had married him for—he took the papers out of her hands, presented them back to the clerk, and said, "She won't need these. This beautiful woman is with me."

He took her by the arm and asked, "So, where are we going to eat?"

"There's a wonderful little place down the street. In walking distance."

Ollie put his arm around her and steered her toward the door as he said, just loud enough for the clerk to overhear, "What did you say your name is?"

Fantasy can add a whole new element of play to "sex play."

Create a fantasy scene together and act it out. Improvise. Fabricate dialogue and action as you each take cues from the other.

Pretend you are:

♦ *well-known celebrities*
♦ *housewife and repairman*
♦ *professional escort and client*
♦ *strangers meeting at a business convention*

Release another whole side of your persona as you have fun playing grown-up make-believe.

———————◆———————

Take a risk and enjoy yourself.

———————◆———————

43. SEXUAL REVERIE

◆ ◆ ◆ ◆ ◆ ◆ ◆ ◆ ◆ ◆ ◆ ◆

Warm up for a steamy night. Recall a particularly enjoyable past sexual experience. Spend a number of minutes lingering over it in your mind. Try to recall as many details as possible. If you have difficulty remembering the particulars, use your imagination to fill in the blanks.

Pick a few of these erotic memories and savor them repeatedly over the course of a day. Having these sexual reveries throughout the day can provide the spark that ignites the fireworks in the evening.

———————◆———————

Stimulate your mind, and your body will follow closely behind.

———————◆———————

44. Share a Fantasy
◆ ◆ ◆ ◆ ◆ ◆ ◆ ◆ ◆ ◆ ◆ ◆ ◆ ◆

"SHARE a fantasy," repeated Rob. "Hmmm . . . I, ah. . . ." He really wanted to play this game with her. Why was it so hard? He choked on a sip of wine, then leaned back on the couch and closed his eyes.

"It's just make-believe. Pretend," Amanda urged gently. "Not something for us to *do*. Just something outrageous that turns you on."

"Well, what if my fantasy turns *you off*?" he said, suddenly realizing part of his concern.

"Then I'll tell you. I mean"—she giggled like a young girl—"I won't go 'Yeeuuughh' real loud or anything. But . . . I'd like to explore . . . our sexuality more." And then she added quietly, "And our vulnerability."

That was when he knew that she was just as nervous as he was. So he took her hand in his, held it on his thigh, and leaned back so that his head rested against the couch. He looked up at the ceiling, then closed his eyes and let the words come out on their own.

"Well, let's see. There's always . . . since I was a kid . . . when I was up in the tree house. I used to dream that Irene Megrey, the older girl who lived next door, would suddenly show up and suck my dick. Right there in the tree house. And then I used to fantasize that sometimes she would have me come to her house while she was sunning herself and ask me to put lotion on her back. And then she would have me put lotion on her front. And then she would put lotion all over me. And we would always end up having sex right there next to her pool."

He got warm and comfortable as he thought about those old fantasies. This wasn't so hard. It was fun. "What about you?"

"Hmm . . ." she said. "Well . . . I know it's weird . . . and I don't think I would like to do this in real life . . . but it keeps coming up as a fantasy . . . and if it's only a fantasy, it really turns me on."

"Yeah?" He squeezed her hand without opening his eyes, just to let her know it was all right to tell him. He was also deeply curious. It had never occurred to him to wonder what her sexual fantasies might be. Or if she even had them.

She almost whispered as she continued. "Well . . . I'm making love to all these guys. But it's not like a gang bang or anything . . . they just adore me. Some of them are kissing me . . . and then one guy will stick his cock inside me. And while he's making love to me, a couple of guys will be standing next to him letting me watch them jerk off. And then . . ."

He was astonished, but didn't want her to stop.

"And then?" he said.

"And then . . . it's just that they are all looking at me with adoration. Like I'm really beautiful. And then one after the other of them gets between my legs and fucks me. Like they really love me. And if I want, I can look over and watch one of the guys making love to this woman next to me. He puts his cock inside her while another guy is making love to me. . . ." She drifted away.

Jeeze . . . he'd never known this about her—this sweet woman he loved so well. He squeezed her hand but didn't want to say anything that would break the spell. He cleared his throat and said, "That's amazing. . . . Ahhh . . . is there more?"

"Yes . . . but now it's your turn."

Amanda stretched out on the couch and put her head in his lap. She could feel his penis hard against her head.

"Okaa-ayy." He stalled, wondering if he should tell her the one that had just popped into his head. His cock got harder and she changed positions so that her cheek rested squarely against it.

She grinned. "Tell me that one." She nuzzled her

face into his crotch and moved her head so that his cock stroked her cheek. "Tell me that one . . . or I won't do anything else . . . ever."

"Okay, okay . . . I'll tell you!"

She nestled her face back down in his lap and waited.

"Well . . . sometimes I have this fantasy that you come to the office . . . and I'm talking on the phone on a business call . . . and you're wearing a trench coat and those high, high heels you have. And you open the coat and you're wearing that short black skirt and the black chiffon blouse, but without the black bra underneath. And I'm still on this phone call and you come around to my side of the desk and bend over it. And while I'm talking to Archie about commodities in China or pork bellies in Kansas, I lift up your skirt and fuck you from behind right there in my office."

"Am I wearing any panties?" Amanda offered, quite pleased with the fantasy.

"No. And it's the corner office, so there's lots of

windows. And sometimes I pretend that there is a helicopter just flying outside the window and these guys are watching me do you. And then you come. And you arch your back and it's just beautiful . . . and poor Archie . . . he knows something's going on, but can't quite figure it out."

Amanda raised her head, then slithered her torso up against him and straddled his lap. "That sounds like a nice fantasy." She looked right into his eyes.

"It does?"

"Uh-huh . . . like something I might like to do sometime."

"Yeah?"

"Uh-huh." She kissed him languorously. "Maybe I'll surprise you." She kissed him again. "But you don't have to arrange for the helicopter."

"Okay."

"*I'll* do that."

He wasn't sure if she was kidding or not, but he

groaned in agreement. Finding out if she was serious was far less important than making love to her right now.

Sharing sexual fantasies with your partner can add variety and excitement to a sexual relationship. First, however, you may want to establish safety by agreeing on some ground rules.

Discuss any aspects of sexuality that, at this point, would not be appealing, even in fantasy.

For example:

◆ *Adding people other than the two of you to the fantasy.*
◆ *Including activities you have never tried together in real life.*

Next, think about areas of your sexual fantasy life that are particularly exciting to you. These may not be activities you would ever want to enact in real life, but ones you find exciting in fantasy.

For example:

- *Being part of a live sex show with crowds of people watching.*
- *Imagining that you are selling sex or buying sex.*
- *Making love with your partner in formal garb after having attended the Academy Awards.*
- *Including a partner of the same sex or a group of people in your lovemaking.*
- *Watching your partner having sex with someone else.*

Choose a fantasy that is sexually exciting to you that falls within the limits of your ground rules. While you verbally spin the fantasy, your partner can physically make love to you. Then switch roles and have your partner fantasize while you do the touching.

◆

Fantasy satisfies a desire for variety or the forbidden. Consequently, the ground rules may change over time.

◆

Why Should Children Have All the Fun?

45. BODY PAINTING

◆ ◆ ◆ ◆ ◆ ◆ ◆ ◆ ◆ ◆ ◆ ◆ ◆ ◆

SHE was exhausted and tense as she approached the front door. It had been a long day. Would Jerry understand if she just sat like a zombie? Too many words. She didn't want to explain anything else to anyone. Not today. As she let herself in, she heard jungle drums from the bedroom. A grin broke across her face. No thinking tonight. Playtime. She dropped her attaché and kicked off her shoes as she headed down the hall toward the bedroom.

When she entered the room he was standing across from her with a washcloth-loincloth held in place by the Western belt she had bought him in Santa Fe. Tribal paint was applied to his forehead and his chest. No talking here. What a relief. She felt a surge of love for this wonderful man and his sense of fun. His way of going beyond the words.

She dropped her clothes to the floor as he walked slowly around her and silently admired her body and its curves. The drums were sweeping her thoughts away in a primeval rush of energy. He dabbed his fingers in a pot of body paint and drew circles on her breasts and around her nipples. Then he traced two bright colored lines down her body, meeting just below her navel. The designs all pointed to and accentuated the power places of a woman . . . the sources of mystery and delight.

And somehow all the turbulent thoughts of the day were left far behind in another world as he kneeled down in front of her and pressed his face silently into her thatch and they spoke the ancestral language—unencumbered by words.

Body painting is a great way to put sex and fun together. Purchase body paint or body paint bubble bath at your local children's store. Use the tubes of bright colors to enhance your partner's physical attributes. And don't just stick to the upper half of the body. Experiment and allow your creativity free reign.

———————◆———————

Sex can be a form of grown-up play.

———————◆———————

46. MÉNAGE À TROIS

Add a vibrator to your sexual experience. There ar
a variety of types to try:

◆ A battery-operated phallus-shaped vibrator is easily
   available and inexpensive, but is often noisy.
◆ An electric plug-in vibrator comes with attachments
   so that it can also be used internally. Some models
   even have a rheostat to control the speed of vibration
◆ The Swedish massager that fits over the hand allow
   fingers to vibrate directly on skin.

Vibrators can be purchased in most large discoun
drugstores or by mail order from magazine adver
tisements. Good Vibrations (415-974-8990) has a
large selection of vibrators.

Choose a vibrator you like, then experiment.
Place your hand on your partner's penis or clitoris
and then press the vibrator on top of your hand,

muting the sensation. Or massage your own genitals directly with the vibrator while your partner stimulates you in other ways. The battery-operated vibrator or the dildo-shaped attachment to the plug-in type can be used inside the vagina or anus. (However, never go from the anus to the vagina without washing the attachment thoroughly.)

See what it's like to have this "third party" join in the lovemaking.

———————◆———————

Individual preferences vary. You may hate one vibrator and love another. So plan to experiment.

———————◆———————

47. TIE AND TEASE

◆ ◆ ◆ ◆ ◆ ◆ ◆ ◆ ◆ ◆ ◆ ◆ ◆ ◆

WELL, when he jokingly mentioned bondage, he didn't really think she would take him up on it. As a matter of fact . . . he was quite surprised when she suggested that she tie *him* up. That's not the way he had envisioned it . . . but fair's fair.

He was a little nervous as he came out of the bathroom, a towel wrapped around his waist. Or was it excitement?

She stood there in her high heels and a bodice that pushed her tits way up and made them look huge. Little panties clung to her hips and were accentuated by black garters that reached down her thighs to fasten the nylons. She looked great. He wanted to jump her right there—and would have, but something in her demeanor told him "no nonsense." Then he noticed the chiffon scarves in her hand as she pointed to the bed.

He lay down on his back. He hadn't felt this unsure about lovemaking since he was a teenager—it was terrific and scary at the same time. She silently took his right hand and, flaunting those gorgeous breasts ever so close to his nose, wrapped a chiffon scarf around his right wrist, moved his arm over his head, and tied the scarf to the brass bed frame.

It wasn't until he was lying spread-eagle on the bed, unable to move his hands and feet, that he began to feel the true extent of his vulnerability. She brought a peacock feather out from nowhere and, without saying a word, began to gently stroke his chest with it. And around his nipples. And down to his navel. And then down to where the towel was still lying across his groin.

She stood next to the bed and gently pulled on the edge of the towel. Somehow this delicate, fragile female had turned into a dominatrix and was now in charge of their lovemaking. The last edge of towel was pulled slowly across his hips to reveal his cock; it sprang to attention. It was as though his penis knew things that he couldn't quite fathom yet.

He watched her gaze down at his dick, standing up like a flagpole. She circled it with the feather and he closed his eyes and let out a groan. When he opened them she was leaning over to lick the smooth shaft. She positioned herself between his spread legs and looked up into his eyes as she took his cock into her mouth. Her tits were practically hanging out of the bustier. He would have pulled his hands away from where they were tied and taken control of the situation right then . . . that is, if he could have. But he couldn't. And he was glad. For all he could do was lie back and enjoy himself. And look down into her eyes while her mouth circled his cock and her tongue explored his balls.

He wanted it to go on forever. And it almost did, for as soon as he got close to orgasm, she would stop and let him cool down before starting something else.

It wasn't until she sat on a chair with her high-heeled feet resting on the edge of the bed that he finally felt the full depth of her eroticism. She opened her legs wide and tilted back in the chair, put two fingers inside the folds of her cunt, and began to move them gently. He watched as her face melted. She looked over at his cock as it stood there quivering all alone, freed her breasts from the bustier, and played with her hard nipples. He watched in fascination and awe.

"I love to look at your hard cock while I play with myself . . ." she whispered.

He watched her fingers explore the deep red folds of her pussy. They slipped in and out. She was losing control. It was as if she didn't care what she looked like anymore . . . only that she woo that illusive orgasm up from inside her.

She took two fingers of her left hand and put them into her vagina. Then, with her right hand, began to press against her clit. Her head fell back with abandon.

"I'm going to come. . . . I want you to watch me come, darling. . . ."

The orgasm poured through her like a rush from the beyond. Her body shuddered and she let out a cry. It seemed to go on and on. And for the first time since he was a kid, he came spontaneously. Just watching her orgasm was enough to make him explode.

When it was all over, she lay down on top of him, loosened his bonds, and freed his hands. He put his arms around her before they both dozed off into sleepy euphoria together.

Playing with bondage can add an element of illicit excitement to your lovemaking.

Choose who will go first and tie that person's wrists and ankles loosely to the bed with ties, scarves, or old stockings. If you have no bedposts, you can safety pin the tethers securely to the mattress. A company called Sports Sheets *makes*

Velcro wrist and ankle bands that can be attached anywhere on the fabric of their sheets.

To ensure that no one gets hurt, pick a word like applesauce or caterpillar—a word you would not normally use—as a way to signal your partner that you really do want to stop. This way you can actually use the words "stop" or "don't" in play without your partner having to worry if you really mean it. Obviously, when the word for stop is signaled, it must always be heeded at once.

Then have fun. Slowly and seductively tease the tied person. Torture your partner with desire. Relish this new forbidden aspect of your sexuality. Create scenarios that excite your imaginations and fantasies.

◆

Experimenting with the forbidden can open new avenues of sexual feelings even if bondage does not turn out to be a turn-on for you or your partner.

◆

EVEN GREAT RELATION- SHIPS HAVE BAD DAYS

48. TALKING

♦ ♦ ♦ ♦ ♦ ♦ ♦ ♦ ♦ ♦ ♦ ♦ ♦ ♦

Change how you handle conflict by using the words "I feel" when talking with your partner.

For example, it is far more effective to say, "I feel unimportant when you make plans for us without checking with me first," rather than, "You are so selfish. You never consider anyone's needs but your own."

A "you" statement is a blaming statement, and will often start or escalate an argument.

An "I" statement directly reports your feelings. This makes you vulnerable. Witnessing your vulnerability encourages your partner to respond in a positive way.

Feelings are expressed by such words as: hurt, unsafe, unloved, lonely, inadequate, happy, loving, *and* invisible.

The feeling must come directly after the phrase "I feel."

For example:

◆ "I feel hurt."
◆ "I feel unimportant."
◆ "I feel unloved."

"I feel that you are . . ." is a blaming statement in disguise.

"I feel as if . . ." is a thinking, not a feeling, statement.

———————◆———————

If you feel angry or frustrated, look for the deeper feeling of hurt or vulnerability that lies beneath the anger or frustration.

———————◆———————

49. LISTENING

◆ ◆ ◆ ◆ ◆ ◆ ◆ ◆ ◆ ◆ ◆ ◆ ◆ ◆

SHE hurried into the restaurant and scanned the tables. Sam was sitting near the patio, fuming. She took off her coat as she hurried over to him.

"I'm sorry I'm late. . . ." She sat down as she talked and beckoned for the waiter to bring her whatever Sam had. "I really am. It couldn't be helped."

Sam sucked in his breath as though he were trying to keep from exploding. "You know, I really feel bad when you're late. It makes me feel unimportant—that our relationship is unimportant to you. It's seven forty-*five*, Linda."

"I can hear how upset you are. I know I'm forty-five minutes late . . . and . . . and I understand how you might feel that I don't really care. . . ." She wanted to say more, but their agreement was to really listen and

mirror the other person's point of view when they dis-
agreed. She bit her tongue and waited.

"I could have spent more time at work. I could have
picked up my dry cleaning. I could have gotten gas . . .
but no, I tore across town because I wanted to be on
time for you. All you had to do was call." He glanced
down at the cellular phone that was lying neatly next to
his fork.

"I understand," she said, trying to keep her
thoughts steady. "I know you have lots of things to do
and I appreciate your effort to be on time. I should
have called, but—" Suddenly she just wanted to cry.
Her thoughts became a jumble and she couldn't
remember the way they had agreed to argue. She just
knew that she loved him and felt bad. "I *wanted* to call
you, but my boss has been standing over my shoulder
for the last three hours shouting changes in the proposal while I keyed them into the computer. We missed

the overnight pickup and he's driving it to the airport himself right now. I'm sorry. I should have called, but . . . I couldn't. I mean . . . I *could* have, but I was overwhelmed and lost track of time."

Somehow, letting it all out cleared her head. She took a breath and really looked at Sam. "I want you to know how much I love you and cherish our relationship. I'll pick up your dry cleaning tomorrow." Then she had a great idea. "Better yet, I'll help you configure your new printer."

His face brightened immediately. The new computer had become his nemesis. "You will?"

She saw his relief and reached for his hand. "Of course I will. What I can't figure out, I'll find out. It'll be up and running by the weekend."

He leaned forward and kissed her, "You're forgiven," he whispered. And they enjoyed a delicious dinner together.

When disagreements arise, many of us are so busy preparing our own replies that we don't really listen to what our partners are saying. To prevent this, do the following:

◆ Limit your statements to just a few sentences at a time.

◆ The person listening must restate in his or her own words what was just said before presenting his or her own point of view.

Both partners alternate back and forth in this manner:

1. She makes a short statement expressing her feelings.
2. He repeats, in his own words, what he heard her say.
3. She agrees with his translation or corrects it.
4. Once it is clear that he has understood what she said, he can then succinctly state his own point of

view (as in number 1), which she then repeats (as in number 2), and so forth.

———◆———

Repeating back what your partner says helps to de-escalate a conflict and makes it easier to attain resolution.

———◆———

50. Conflict Resolution

♦ ♦ ♦ ♦ ♦ ♦ ♦ ♦ ♦ ♦ ♦ ♦ ♦ ♦ ♦

"You know," she shouted angrily, "just because I love you doesn't mean I have to agree with you."

She stood in the middle of the living room with her hands on her hips staring at him. He sat in the big gray chair staring back at her, stunned. He was really pissed at her, but didn't want to get into a fight. As a matter of fact, he just wanted to get back to his reading. Let it all blow over. He didn't say anything, which said a lot.

She continued. "I really understand the pressure you are under and I think you are doing fabulous under the circumstances . . . but I am really upset right now. And I feel ignored."

He was finding it hard to contain himself. He *didn't* want to talk about this or anything else right now. Not until she cooled down and came to her senses.

Then she did the strangest thing he had ever seen. She started to sing. Loud. And angry. To the tune of "You Are So Beautiful," she practically shouted out:

> You're such an imbecile . . . to me. . . .
> Why don't you talk to me . . . and see. . . .
> How much fun . . . I—I can be. . . .
>
> You ignored me during lunchtime,
> You took a book and read . . .
>
> I felt so stupid . . . just sitting there . . .

He just stared at her, speechless. He couldn't just burst into song in his own living room. Particularly when he was mad. He thought a moment and saw her eyes brimming with tears, then took a deep breath. He actually sang pretty poorly, kind of off key, but he liked to think he was approximating "Bridge over Troubled Water."

> Like a man swimming in troubled water,
> Won't you give me some help?
> I have all this reading to do by Monday . . .
> I'm afraid I'll get fired if I don't. . . .

He got really off key and way out of meter, and pretty soon he was wandering around in some unintelligible melody like a German opera singer. But he didn't care; he was on a roll.

> You think you're the only one with feelings.
> Well, I have feee-lings . . . too!
> And I feel pretty scared right now,
> That's why I don't have time for yoouu. . . .

He actually didn't know what else to sing. Or say, for that matter. Neither did she. She was so shocked by his reply that she just stood there. Then she felt the impulse to sing simply and quietly, "You are so beautiful to me. . . ."

They stood there and just looked at each other for another moment. She came close and kissed him on the cheek. He let her. Then he took her face in his hands and kissed her very sincerely. Before the kiss could get serious and time-consuming, he turned his attention back to his book. She gave him a quick peck in return, brought him a good reading light, and went downstairs to check out "www.eroticfilms.com" on the Internet.

To resolve the next conflict, do the following:

♦ *Presume your partner to be innocent. This is essential. We are all innocent until proven guilty.*

♦ *Be "curious" rather than "furious." Try to under-*

stand your partner's actions from his or her point of view—which is likely to be very different from your own, yet equally valid.

♦ Find the "grain of truth" in what your partner is saying—the part that you can agree with. Then acknowledge the part you agree with before explaining your perspective on the situation.

———————♦———————

Remember, just because you understand your partner's position doesn't mean you need to back down on your own point of view. Both perspectives may be valid and true.

———————♦———————

EPILOGUE

THE major difference between those couples who maintain a passionate sex life over the years and those who don't is time.

We all have busy lives. Having time to do *everything* is not possible. Look at the choices you make. If you want your sexual relationship to be a source of fun, excitement, and pleasure, you need to prioritize it. Plan for it. Look forward to it. Relish it. Otherwise it won't happen. It will get lost in the busy schedule of life.

If you indulged in one of the activities in this book each week for (almost) a year—every year—you could die really happy.

ACKNOWLEDGMENTS

50 *Ways to Please Your Lover* has had a number of incarnations. It was inspired by my work with The Venus Group and the videotape-audiotape-workbook program for sexual enhancement that we put together titled *Falling in Love Again*. (For more information on this program, call 800-228-4630.)

Carole DeSanti, my editor at Dutton, gets significant credit for the final form of this book. Seven renditions and two years later only three pages of the original draft remain. I could never have done it without Carole's help.

I would also like to thank my agent, Rhoda Weyr, for her continued support, and my assistant, Marilyn Anderson, for her infinite flexibility, intelligence, and delightful disposition.

Finally, I am indebted to David Geisinger and Tess

Geisinger-Barbach for all of the many ways they bring pleasure into each and every day of my life. My life would be seriously diminished without them. In addition, David is responsible for both the titles and concepts that underlie a number of the activities.

"Ingredients for Great Sex" was developed by Bernie Zilbergeld, Ph.D., author of *The New Male Sexuality*.

"Upside/Downside," "Foreplay," and "Conflict Resolution" come from *Going the Distance: Finding and Keeping Lifelong Love* by Lonnie Barbach, Ph.D., and David Geisinger, Ph.D.

"Caring Days" is borrowed from the work of Richard Stuart, D.S.W.